A Glossary & of Grammar Linguistics

A Glossary of Grammar & of Grammar & Linguistics

Andrew MacLeish

Originally published as Part II of Modern English

I.C.C. LIBRARY

The Universal Library
GROSSET & DUNLAP, INC.
A NATIONAL GENERAL COMPANY
New York

A Grosset & Dunlap Original
Universal Library Edition, 1972
Originally published as Part II of Modern English

A
Glossary
&of Grammar
Linguistics

A Note About This Glossary

This glossary of English grammar and linguistics is for the beginning student. The descriptions are of terms and topics as they are used in their most frequent and familiar senses in beginning and intermediate courses in the field. The main concern of this glossary is with facts about grammar and linguistics; thus the terms are not labeled as to their parts of speech, and pronunciations are not given. Frequently, though not with complete consistency, the terms have been treated in their noun forms.

In one sense this is more than a glossary, for there is a good deal of encyclopedic description, information about the referent rather than merely a description of words. The list includes, then, not only terms but also topics (DISTINCTIVE FEATURES), events (THE FIRST CONSONANT SHIFT), and laws (VERNER'S LAW). The subject orientation is toward language history, phonemics, dialects, and grammar with much the heaviest emphasis on the latter, since it is the most frequent aspect of linguistics in school and college curricula. One of the major purposes of this glossary is, wherever possible, to contrast descriptions from the three grammars that receive most attention in introductory courses: conventional school grammar and structural and transformational grammars. Such items as ADJECTIVE and RULE OF GRAMMAR are thus defined from three points of view. Several models of transformational grammar are suggested in the description of terms. An effort has been made to treat those models that are found in textbooks available at the time of composition of the glossary. Thus, while there is consideration of early terms and models, there is also an attempt to reflect more recent systems.

Symbols and Abbreviations

Because some of the terms in this glossary are defined from the point of view of more than one kind of grammar, these three abbreviations are used throughout: *CG*: As defined in conventional school grammar; *Str*: As defined in structural grammar; *TG*: As defined in transformational grammar.

Listed below are the conventional symbols and abbreviations used in this glossary, with accompanying explanations.

↔   "agreement between subject and verb." EXAMPLE: N ↔ V

→   (1) "can be rewritten as/expanded into." EXAMPLE: S → NP + VP means "Sentence can be rewritten as/expanded into Noun Phrase + Verb Phrase."
(2) This arrow is also used in the more traditional sense of "becomes." EXAMPLE: Indo-European *bh* → Germanic *b*

⇒   "can be transformed into." EXAMPLE: NP + V + Pred ⇒ V + NP + Pred means "the order of the string of symbols to the left of the arrow is transformed into the order of the string of symbols to the right of the arrow"

( )   When this parenthesis appears in a rule of grammar it means "the element inside the parenthesis is optional; you do not have to choose it." EXAMPLE: S → NP + VP (Adv) means "Sentence is rewritten as Noun Phrase + Verb Phrase + an optional adverb"

{ }   (1) In a syntactic rule this means "choose one of the obligatory elements inside the braces." EXAMPLE:

$$N \rightarrow \begin{Bmatrix} N_{pr} \\ N_{com} \end{Bmatrix}$$

means "nouns are either proper or common; you must choose either one or the other, but not both at the same time."
(2) Morphemes are placed within braces. EXAMPLE: $\{-s_2\}$ means "plural morpheme"

[ ]   (1) In a syntactic rule this means "the elements within brackets share the element that follows." EXAMPLE:

$$\begin{bmatrix} stay \\ remain \end{bmatrix} + Predicate$$

means "both *stay* and *remain* can be followed by a predicate."
(2) Brackets enclose phonetic transcription. EXAMPLE: $[p^h]$.
(3) Brackets enclose a list of distinctive features. EXAMPLE:

walk

$$\begin{bmatrix} +VB \\ +V \\ +action \end{bmatrix}$$

⟨ ⟩	Angle brackets are used to enclose graphemes and single distinctive features. EXAMPLES: ⟨a⟩ ⟨+VB⟩
*	(1) Preceding a sentence, the asterisk means that the sentence is unacceptable. EXAMPLE: *What ignored Joe was Mary. (2) Preceding a word or the transcription of a word, the asterisk indicates a hypothetical or reconstructed form. EXAMPLES: Primitive Germanic* [bro: θer]; Indo-European *kmtom
‾	When the macron is over a written symbol, usually a vowel, it means length. EXAMPLE: habēre
:	After a transcribed vowel, the colon means full length. EXAMPLE: [e:]
↑	Rising intonation. EXAMPLE: Is she here ↑
↓	Falling intonation. EXAMPLE: She's here ↓
→	Level intonation. EXAMPLE: She's a nice girl → but. . . .
~	Phonologically conditioned alternation
∞	Morphologically conditioned alternation
Adj	Adjective
Adv	Adverb
Af	Affix. EXAMPLE: Noun + Af = Boy + s
ART	Article
AUX	Auxiliary verb
C	TG: Complement construction following a verb. EXAMPLE: likes living there
CG	Conventional school grammar
(COMP)/ (N-COMP)	TG: The open position after a noun which can be filled by a transformed insert sentence which modifies the noun
COMP	CG: The complement of the verb
D/Det	Determiner. EXAMPLE: a, the, several of the, many of the
{-d₁}	The past tense morpheme
DO	Direct Object
ed/en	The past tense morpheme as it is represented in the terminal string of a phrase structure grammar
ing	The progressive aspect morpheme
IO	Indirect Object
LOC(ATIVE)	An adverb of location. EXAMPLE: there, at the corner
LV	Linking Verb
M	Modal Auxiliary
MOT	Adverb of motion. EXAMPLE: ran into the house
MV	Main Verb
N	Noun
N°	Number; either singular or plural
N_human	Human noun. EXAMPLE: man, boy, girl

NEG	Negative particle. EXAMPLE: *not, 'nt*
Nom	Nominal
NP	Noun Phrase
OV	Object complement verb. EXAMPLE: *elected* Bob President
PRE-ART	Pre-article. EXAMPLE: *some of, all of, many of*
Pred	Predicate
s	The plural morpheme in a string
S	Sentence
$\{-s_2\}$	the noun plural morpheme
Str.	Structural Grammar
TG	Transformational Grammar
V	Verb
V_b	Any other verb besides BE in the rule

$$MV \rightarrow \left\{ \begin{matrix} BE + Predicate \\ V_b \end{matrix} \right\}$$

V_{be}	The verb *be*
V_c	Any linking verb except *be*
V_i/V_{int}	Intransitive verb
V_{iL}/V_L	Verbs like *sit* that are usually followed by adverbials of location EXAMPLE: sit *at the table*
V_{iM}	Verbs like *run* that are usually followed by adverbials of motion EXAMPLE: run *into the house*
V_t/V_{tr}	Transitive verb
VP	Verb Phrase
Ø	(1) A morphologically conditioned allomorph. EXAMPLE: plural of *sleep, deer* (2) No suffix

The Phonemic Transcription

The phonemic transcription used in this glossary is a very slightly modified version of the Pike-Fries system found on pages 450–51. The pronunciations are those of most northern dialects of American English. See pages 401–2.

VOWELS

/i/	beat				
/ɪ/	bit	/ɨ/	candid	/u/	too
/e/	bait	/ər/	sir, butter	/ʊ/	put
/ɛ/	bet	/ə/	but	/o/	note
/æ/	bat	/a/	pot	/ɔ/	law

CONSONANTS

Stops		Affricates		Fricatives		Nasals		Lateral	
/p/	pin	/č/	church	/f/	fan	/m/	met	/l/	live
/b/	bin	/ĵ/	jump	/v/	van	/n/	net		
/t/	tin			/θ/	thin	/ŋ/	ring		
/d/	din			/ð/	then				
/k/	kin			/s/	sip				
/g/	give			/z/	zip				
				/š/	ship				
				/ž/	rouge				
				/h/	help				

GLIDES
/r/   run
/y/   yes
/w/   win

DIPHTHONGS
/ai/   sigh
/au/   how
/ɔi/   boy

In addition, two symbols are included in the historical entries which represent sounds no longer in English:

/x/   voiceless velar fricative as in German "Nacht," "Buch"; the closest approximation in English is the initial sound in "cool"

/ɣ/   voiced velar fricative. The same sound as /x/ except it is voiced. It is similar to /g/ except that it has friction. It is the medial g in Spanish rogar

ablaut   The changes that occur in a vowel sound as a result of variations in pitch in the parent language and in the stress accent of languages that evolve from this parent language. The vowel thus goes through a series of changes. *Nest,* for example, is ultimately related to Indo-European **nizdo,* "sitting-down place." The prefix *ni-* means "down" and *-zd-* is related to Germanic *-st-.* The vowel *o* was lost because of lack of stress in Indo-European, leaving *nizd,* which appears in Germanic languages as *nest.* Verb forms such as *ring, rang, rung* and *strike, streak, stroke, stricken* are evidences of ablaut, a series of vowel changes. (See GRADATION.)

absolute construction   This is composed of a noun in the common case, or a pronoun in nominative or objective case, followed by a nonfinite verb or an adjectival. This construction has no syntactic relationship with the rest of the sentence but serves as a sentence modifier. Examples:

> *His hand in a sling,* he grabbed the beer.
> *Her arm being broken,* she wore it in a sling.
> *The work being completed,* we went home.
> *He being boss,* I did what he said.
> We felt sad, *the house having collapsed.*
> He kissed Matilda, *his face sorrowful.*

abstract noun   *CG:* A noun that names a quality, condition, action, or anything that cannot be perceived by the senses: *love, sickness, running, justice. Str:* Abstract nouns generally do not take the plural suffix. Some of them pattern in the singular without the determiner:

_____ is common.

TG: An abstract noun names an abstract quality. Most of these nouns can occur in subject position opposite a noun clause or noun phrase in a sentence with the verb *be:*

> *Opposite Noun Clause:*   The *problem* is that I don't know him.
> *Opposite Noun Phrase:*   *Happiness* is to love.

(See LEXICAL PROPERTIES.)

accidence   A term describing changes in the form of a word when it is inflected for gender (*he/she*), number (*boy/boys*), case (*I/me*), tense (*burn/burned*). (See CONJUGATION, DECLENSION, INFLECTION, PARADIGM.)

accusative A term from the grammar of classical languages designating the word that is the object of the verb. English has six distinctive pronoun forms that are used as objects: *me, her, him, us, them,* and, less frequently, *whom.* Since nouns have no distinctive forms to show that they are the objects of verbs and prepositions, this function is indicated in English by word order. But nominal direct objects are sometimes called accusative. (See CASE, DIRECT OBJECT, OBJECT.)

acoustic phonetics The study of significant speech sounds as they are heard by the listener. (Compare with ARTICULATORY PHONETICS: see DISTINCTIVE FEATURES.)

REFERENCES: N. Chomsky and M. Halle, *The Sound Pattern of English* (New York: Harper & Row, 1968); M. Halle, "On the Bases of Phonology," in J. A. Fodor and J. J. Katz (eds.), *The Structure of Language, Readings in the Philosophy of Language* (Englewood Cliffs: Prentice-Hall, 1964); _____, "Phonology in Generative Grammar," in *ibid.;* R. T. Harms, *Introduction to Phonological Theory* (Englewood Cliffs: Prentice-Hall, 1968); R. Jakobson and M. Halle, *Fundamentals of Language* ('s-Gravenhage: Mouton, 1956); _____, C. G. M. Fant, and M. Halle, *Preliminaries to Speech Analysis* (Cambridge, Mass.: MIT Acoustics Laboratory, 1952); P. Postal, *Aspects of Phonological Theory* (New York: Harper & Row, 1968); B. M. H. Strang, *Modern English Structure,* 2nd ed. (New York: St. Martin's Press, 1968).

active voice When the subject of the verb is the actor or is in a condition named by the verb, the verb is said to be in the active voice.

> *Actor:* Bill threw the ball.
> *Condition:* He slept for eight hours.

actor-action-goal construction A grammatical construction in which the order of words indicates their grammatical relationships. *John scared the dog* and *The dog scared John* both show the same grammatical action, but actor and goal in the second construction signal a reversed meaning.

additive allomorph The allomorph of a suffix added to a base. The past-tense morpheme {-d₁} has three phonologically conditioned allomorphs that are additive: /-ɨd~ -d ~-t/ are added to bases to form /sitɨd simd læft/. The plural morpheme {-s₂} has three phonologically conditioned allomorphs and two morphologically conditioned allomorphs, all of which are additive; /-ɨz~ -z~ -s∞ ɨn~∅/ are added to bases to form the plurals /bičɨz dɔgz kæts aksɨn šip/. (See ALLOMORPH, MORPHOLOGICAL CONDITIONING, PHONOLOGICAL CONDITIONING, REPLACIVE ALLOMORPH.)

adjective *CG:* A word used to limit, describe, or qualify a noun or noun equivalent. *Str:* Adjectives, when used in comparison, can be inflected with *-er* or *-est.* The base form of most polysyllabic adjectives, when they are used in comparison, is preceded by *more* or *most,* in which case there is no inflection. Adjectives pattern between the article and the noun modified or after nouns as part of larger constructions:

a *larger* house
a house *larger* than I thought

Predicate adjectives follow *be* and linking verbs. *TG:* In one model of this grammar an adjective is a modifier derived from a transformed insert sentence that is embedded into a matrix sentence:

Matrix: Joe is a man (COMP).
Transformed Insert: Joe is old ⟹ who is old ⟹ who is old
Embedded Result: Joe is an old man.

In a more recent model of this grammar adjectives are considered to be in some ways similar to verbs in the DEEP STRUCTURE of sentences. They are, thus, verbals that are marked ⟨+VB⟩ and ⟨−V⟩. (See INSERT SENTENCE; LEXICAL PROPERTIES; VERBAL.)

adjectival   An adjective, noun, participle, adverb, or syntactic construction that is in a shared position usually filled by adjectives:

Adjective:	*green* house
Noun:	*telephone* office
Participle:	*burning* house
	burned steak
Adverb:	the *upstairs* room
Syntactic Construction:	*very old* man

(See POSITION CLASS.)

adjective clause   A clause that occurs after a noun and modifies it:

car *that I drove*

(See RELATIVE CLAUSE.)

adjective complement   Another term for PREDICATE ADJECTIVE.

adverb   *CG:* An adverb modifies, describes, or limits a verb, adverb, or adjective. *Str:* Many adverbs are adjectives or participles plus the ending *-ly: poorly, dashingly.* Like adjectives, adverbs can be compared with *-er, -est* or *more, most.* They express such concepts as time, place, degree, manner, and number, and they can occur in various positions in a sentence without changing its meaning. Some frequent positions occupied by adverbs in English are before the sentence (*Now* it's time to run.), after the subject (He *actually* thinks about it.), after the auxiliary or first auxiliary (I will *seldom* eat that.), after the verb (He drives *recklessly.* She is *always* a lady.), after the Subject Complement (He will be pitcher *tomorrow.*), after the Object Complement (He will be elected captain *tomorrow.*), after the Direct Object (He will play baseball *tomorrow.*). (See PRO-FORM.)

adverb clause   A dependent clause modifying a verb, adverb, adjective, or sentence. It expresses notions such as time, place, cause, manner, concession, condition, comparison, purpose, and result.

> *Verb Modifier:* I will go *when I am ready.*
> *Adverb Modifier:* He runs faster *than Joe does.*
> *Adjective Modifier:* She is younger *than her sister is.*
> *Sentence Modifier:* *When he is ready,* we'll go to town.

adverbial   This term describes single words, phrases, and clauses that fill adverb positions in sentences.

> *Single Word:* He fell *down.*
> *Phrase:* He fell *down the stairs.*
> *Clause:* He fell *while he was running.*

affix   A general term describing bound morphemes that are prefixes (*re*-run), infixes (man:men), or suffixes (quick*ly*). (See BOUND MORPHEME, MORPHEME.)

affix transformation   An obligatory transformation upon a terminal string. It rearranges affixes (Af) and verbs (V) within the auxiliary:

$$\text{Af} + \text{V} \Rightarrow \text{V} + \text{Af}:$$

en + break ⇒ broken
ed + burn ⇒ burned
s + break ⇒ breaks
ing + break ⇒ breaking
Ø + can ⇒ can

where Af = -en, -ed, -s (third singular present tense), -ing, Ø (zero affix on modal auxiliaries). Here is an illustration of how this transformation operates on a terminal string:

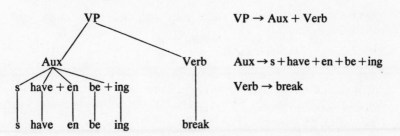

VP → Aux + Verb

Aux → s + have + en + be + ing

Verb → break

After the obligatory affix transformation has been applied, the result is

has been breaking

(See OBLIGATORY TRANSFORMATION, SIMPLE TRANSFORMATION, TERMINAL STRING.)

affricate   A meaningful sound consisting of two types of articulation, a stop followed by a fricative. English has a voiceless affricate /č/, the first and last sounds in *church,* and a voiced affricate /ǰ/, the first sound in Jim.

agglutinative language   A language like Swahili, Hungarian, or Turkish, in which words are made up of parts that are whole syllables and have lexical meanings. Affixes are attached to invariable and independent bases. Consider Swahili *atanipenda,* "he will like me," *atakupenda* "he will like you," *atanipiga* "he will beat me," where the affixes have lexical meaning: *ata = he; ni = me; ku = you; penda = like; piga = beat.* Contrast this with English *books,* in which the base *book* has lexical meaning, but the affix *s* means plural and is not a syllable.

agnate   *TG:* Sentences that are agnate have a traceable relationship. *I saw the man* and *The man ran away* combine to form *I saw the man who ran away.* They combine, are related, through a series of transformational rules, thus they are agnate.

agreement   *CG:* Sometimes called *concord,* this is a formal correspondence between two parts of speech. Subject and verb agree in number:

He is here.
They are there.

Demonstrative pronouns generally agree in number with the nouns they precede:

this dog
those shoes

Pronouns agree in number and gender with their noun antecedents:

Number: I saw the *planes* and liked *them.*
Gender : I saw *Mary* and liked *her.*

allomorph   One of the related forms that belong to the same morpheme. These related forms have the same meaning and are in complementary distribution. For example, the past tense morpheme {-d₁} has the phonologically conditioned allomorphs /-d/: rubb*ed;* /-t/: stopp*ed;* /ɨd/: heat*ed.* (See ADDITIVE ALLOMORPH, COMPLEMENTARY DISTRIBUTION, MORPHEME, REPLACIVE ALLOMORPH.)

allophone   One of the individual sounds comprising a phoneme; a positional variant of a phoneme. For example, [kʰ], the initial sound in *king,* and [k⁼], the final sound in *book,* are, respectively, aspirated and unaspirated allophones of /k/. Aspiration is a puff of air that can follow the articulation of any consonant sound.

alveolar stop   A significant speech sound. English has two: /t/ and /d/. (See STOP.)

ambiguity   Two or more meanings in a word or construction. Ambiguities are either lexical or structural. In lexical ambiguity the multiple meaning is in the words themselves:

The Reverend Smith was congratulated on getting his *parish plastered.*

Structural ambiguity results from a mistake in the structure—the arrangement of words—of an utterance or written sentence:

Her thoughts were interrupted as the door swung open and a young woman carrying a baby and her husband entered.

REFERENCE: N. C. Stageberg, "Some Structural Ambiguities," in H. B. Allen (ed.), *Readings in Applied English Linguistics,* rev. ed. (New York: Appleton-Century-Crofts, 1964).

analogy   This is the name for the natural, unconscious tendency among speakers to make their language more regular than it may be. New words are formed by the same processes that have formed existing ones, "irregular" constructions are regularized into more frequently occurring patterns. An example of the first process is the Anglicization of plurals of Latin words into English plurals: *stadium-stadiums.* Past-tense forms of "irregular" verbs are frequently analogized to regular *-ed* forms: *drive-drived.* Analogy is a powerful and intuitive force in the process of language change.

analytic language   One in which the relationships among words, thus their functions, depend upon the order of words and the use of prepositions and auxiliary verbs. Modern English is an analytic language, as is French. Modern German, Latin, and Old English are SYNTHETIC LANGUAGES. (See INFLECTIONAL LANGUAGE, SYNTHETIC LANGUAGE.)

Anglo-Saxon   A highly inflected ancestor language of Modern English spoken in the British Isles in the period c. A.D. 500–1000.

REFERENCES: A. Campbell, *Old English Grammar* (Oxford: Clarendon Press, 1959), J. W. Clark, *Early English* (New York: Norton, 1957); S. Moore and T. A. Knott, *The Elements of Old English,* 8th ed. (Ann Arbor: Wahr, 1940); R. Quirk and C. L. Wrenn, *An Old English Grammar,* 2nd ed. (London: Methuen, 1958).

animate noun   *CG:* Animate nouns name living things: *dog, man, boy,* etc. *TG:* Animate nouns are a subclass of concrete nouns. Those nouns that must occur as subjects with such verbs as *breathe* and *play. Dog, man, boy, poet* are animate nouns. (See LEXICAL PROPERTIES.)

anomolous verbs   *Be, go, do,* and *will* are called anomolous verbs because their forms come from different verbs rather than from one.

Be has forms from three Old English infinitives: *beon, is,* and *wesan; go* used the preterit *ēode* but now employs *went,* the preterit of *wend.*

antecedent   That word or group of words to which a pronoun refers.

I saw *Fred* while *he* was at home.   *To see Fred again; that* excites me.

apocope   The loss of a final sound during the process of language change. For example, Old English *singan* became Modern English *sing.*

apposition   Two constructions or words that are next to each other and refer to the same person or thing.

Our teacher, Mr. Smith, is a good one.

appositive   The second of two words or constructions in apposition is usually called the appositive. In the example above, *Mr. Smith* is the appositive.

archaism   A word, construction, or expression that is in infrequent current use and is recognized as being from an earlier period of the language. Examples are *forsooth, durst* (for *dared*).

argot   The name given to words and expressions that are peculiar to a particular class or group, mainly in the criminal underworld. The term was originally used in the nineteenth century to describe the talk of thieves who wished to disguise or conceal meanings. It still describes criminal language such as *yellow* (a telegram), *apple* (the victim), *to light a rag* (to run away), *to play the C* (to operate a confidence game).

article   *The* is the definite article; *a, an* are indefinite articles. Articles are frequently considered a subclass of adjectives. (See DETERMINER.)

articulative intrusion   The process by which sounds are added to words at any time during their course of development or use. These additional sounds come into words as a result of the mechanics of articulation. (See INTRUSIVE CONSONANT.)

articulatory phonetics   The study of the production of speech sounds. This study is based upon the manner of production and points of articulation of speech sounds, and establishes classifications among these sounds. (See ACOUSTIC PHONETICS, AFFRICATE, CONSONANT, FRICATIVE, GLIDE, LATERAL, STOP, VOWEL.)

REFERENCES: A. Bronstein, *The Pronunciation of American English* (New York: Appleton-Century-Crofts, 1960); C. F. Hockett, *A Manual of Phonology* (Baltimore: Williams and Wilkins, 1955); J. S. Kenyon, *American Pronunciation,* 10th ed. (Ann Arbor: Wahr, 1950); H. Kurath, *A Phonology and Prosody of Modern English* (Ann Arbor: University of Michigan Press, 1964); G. L. Trager and H. L. Smith, Jr., *An Outline of English Structure* (Washington: ACLS, 1963 [reprint]).

aspect   A term sometimes used to describe the nature of the action of a verb. Aspect does not refer to the time of an action but rather to whether the action is completed (punctual aspect):

I wrote. I had written.

is not yet completed (durative or progressive aspect):

I am writing.

has recently begun (inchoative aspect):

He got going.
Let's get moving.

is repeated (repetitive aspect):

We keep moving from house to house.

or is emphasized (emphatic aspect):

He did *too* win it.

(See PROGRESSIVE TENSE.)

aspiration   A puff of air, represented by /ʰ/, that can follow the articulation of any consonant sound. Aspiration is not phonemic in English; it is a predictable allophonic feature of the voiceless stop consonants /p t k/ in certain positions. For example, these three consonants are aspirated in initial positions before a vowel: *pin* /pʰɪn/, *tin* /tʰɪn/, *can* /kʰæn/. In final word position, aspiration is a nonpredictable allophonic feature in free variation with lack of aspiration in the same phoneme: *lap* /læpʰ/ or /læp/; *rat* /rætʰ/ or /ræt/; *lack* /lækʰ/ or læk/. The glottal fricative /ʰ/ does not follow another consonant phoneme before a vowel and thus does not represent phonemic aspiration. Some English words spelled with initial *ph* (*photo*), *th* (*Thomas*), and *kh* (*khaki*) probably reflect aspirated initial consonants in the languages from which they were borrowed or an analogy with which they were spelled: Greek, Latin, Hindi.

assimilation   The phonetic process by which one sound changes to resemble or become identical with a sound near it. There are two kinds of assimilation: voice assimilation and place assimilation. (1) Voice assimilation occurs when a sound becomes voiced or voiceless to resemble one of the sounds surrounding it. The word *north* ends with a voiceless *th*. When we add *ern* to *north, northern,* the *th* becomes a voiced sound to resemble the voiced sound, *er,* which now follows it. This is also known as phonological conditioning. (2) Place assimilation is of two kinds. (*a*) In the first, two sounds come to resemble each other in that they are articulated in the same part of the mouth. The two pronunciations spelled *strength* and *strenth* illustrate this. The sound of *ng* in the first pronunciation comes to resemble the sound of *n* in the second. The second one is easier to pronounce because both the *n* and the *th* are articulated in the front of the mouth. In *ngth*, the tongue is in the back of the mouth for *ng* and moves to the front of the mouth for *th*. In *strenth*, then, we have a pronunciation shortcut; the sound of *ng* has been assimilated to, has been made like, the sound of *n*. (*b*) In the second, one sound becomes identical with another. An example of this can be found in the pronunciation of *horseshoe*. The usual pronunciation might be spelled *horshoe*. Here the final *s* of *horse* is assimilated to, has become identical with, the *sh* sound of *shoe*. This standard pronunciation is a shortcut; it reduces the movements of the tongue from two to one at this point in the pronunciation of the word.

attribute   *CG:* The same as a HEADWORD.

attributive   *CG:* An adjective in position before or after a noun: *small* house; house *dark* and *dreary*. A noun modifying another noun is used attributively: *telephone* operator.

auxiliary verb   Sometimes called a helping verb; the term describes a verb used with the infinitive or participial form of the main verb to form a verb phrase. *Be, do* and *have* are used most frequently as auxiliary verbs:

> I *am* going.
> I *didn't* want it.
> He *has* gone.

Can, could, may, shall, will, must, should, would, might, and *ought* (*to*) are also frequent in this use in American English. *TG:* In this grammar, auxiliary material includes tense, which is obligatory, plus optional modals and/or *have* and/or *be*. The auxiliary rule can be written this way:

$$\text{Aux} \rightarrow \text{Tense (Modal) (have - ed) (be - ing)}$$

This rule accounts for all sixteen active voice auxiliary phrases in English. (See VERB PHRASE.)

B

back formation   A process of word formation that is the reverse of the usual method in English. It is the formation of a word from one that looks like its derivative. Centuries ago the verbs *peddle* and *beg* were formed from the nouns *peddlar* and *beggar*. The modern verb *televise* has been back-formed from the noun *television* on the analogy with pairs such as *supervise-supervision, revise-revision.* (See ANALOGY.)

back vowel   A vowel articulated at the back of the mouth. (See VOWEL.)

base   A term used in the study of morphemes. A *base* morpheme is the one that carries the principal meaning in structures like *cat*s, *friend*ly. Bases are of two kinds: free and bound. Most bases in English are free; they can occur alone. *Cat* and *friend* are free bases. Many bound bases in English come from Latin and Greek; they can occur in English only with affixes. Thus, they are bound to affixes and cannot occur alone. The italicized bound bases in the following words illustrate this: *dict*ate, contra*dict,* in*spect, spect*acles; *port*able, re*port;* in*spire,* re*spire.*

base form   When the linguist wishes to make statements about the variations, or allomorphs, of a morpheme, he chooses one allomorph as the base form and considers the others as describable variations of it. Thus the English noun plural morpheme $\{-s_2\}$ has three phonologically conditioned allomorphs $/-z \sim -s \sim -\dot{+}z/$ (son*s*, cake*s*, glass*es*), any one of which might be considered as the base form at a given time.

base rules   Base rules are one of the two types of syntactic rules that relate deep structure and surface structure. Base rules are rewrite rules of the form

$$S \rightarrow NP + VP$$

and they are represented by a tree diagram:

In relating surface structure with its meaning, its deep structure, base rules function in several ways. The elements of the surface structure

$$the + man + feed + PAST + the + dog$$

are arranged one after the other, in linear order, by base rules. Changing this linear order yields an ungrammatical surface structure such as

$$dog + the + the + PAST + feed + man$$

or a sentence which differs from the original:

the + dog + feed + PAST + the + man

In addition, base rules group elements together to form units of meaning like *the + man, feed + PAST*, and *feed + PAST + the + dog*. Two other functions of base rules can be understood by looking at this tree diagram:

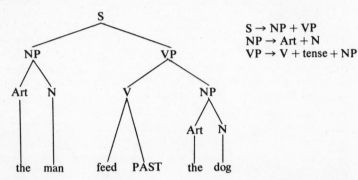

$$S \rightarrow NP + VP$$
$$NP \rightarrow Art + N$$
$$VP \rightarrow V + tense + NP$$

As native speakers of English we can intuitively group these elements in units like *the + man* and *feed + PAST + the + dog*. But these groupings do not show what kind of units, constituents, these sequences are. The labelled node points (S, NP, VP, etc.) show us what kind of constituent a given group is. The shape of the tree diagram is prescribed by the base rules to the right of it which, then, label the constituents. The base rules also group constituents into related hierarchies of varying size. The constituents *V* and *NP* (*feed + PAST* and *the dog*), for example, are parts of the larger constituent *VP* which is itself a constituent of *S*. Consider a more complicated diagram:

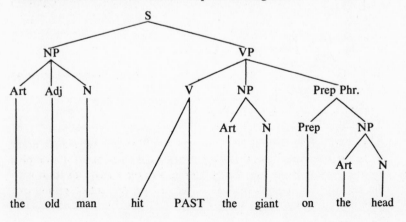

This diagram illustrates another function of base rules—they account for similar constituents of varying complexity. We see that *the giant* and *the old man* can function as noun phrases as can even more complex structures like *the old man who lives down the street*. Similarly, a verb phrase can be a single word like *hit* or it may be more complex like *hit the giant* or *hit the giant on the head*. All of these constituents are labelled either NPs or VPs because they function as noun phrases or verb phrases. Though some are more complex than others, they are all governed by the same sets of base rules for NPs and VPs. In relating deep and surface structures, then, base rules arrange morphemes in a linear order, group elements together into meaningful units, label the constituents in a tree diagram, group constituents into related hierarchies of varying size, and account for the similarity of constituents of varying complexity. (See PHRASE STRUCTURE RULES, REWRITE RULE, RULE OF GRAMMAR, TREE DIAGRAM.)

be-verb   The verb *be* comprises a single-member class. Syntactically, it is similar to the transitive verb, the mid-verb, and *become, stay,* and *remain* in that all of them can be followed by a noun phrase. It is most like *become, stay,* and *remain* since the predicate noun phrase of both must refer to the same person or thing as the subject:

Become: The man became chairman.
Be: The man is chairman.

Be also resembles linking verbs in that both can be followed by a predicate adjective that modifies the subject; but linking verbs can be followed only by adjectivals:

Linking Verb: The man appeared strong.
Be: The man is strong.

Be is like intransitive verbs in that both can be immediately followed by an adverbial:

Intransitive Verb: The boy sleeps in the bed.
Be: The boy is in the bed.

Be is different from the intransitive verb, however, in that *be* must be followed by a completing element:

Intransitive Verb: The boy sleeps.
Be: *The boy is.

Be has at least seven forms: I *am;* you, we, they *are;* ne, she, it, noun *is.* In the past tense the singular form is *was,* plural *were.* Participles are the present *being* and the past *been. Ain't* is a frequent form with the negative. Infrequent archaic forms are the present thee/thou *art,* past indicative thee/thou *wast,* and past subjunctive thee/thou *wert.*

Be is an auxiliary verb as well as a full, or main, verb. (See AUXILIARY VERB.)

bilabial stop   A consonant made by a momentary stoppage, then release, of air by the lips. (See STOP.)

binary construction   *SG:* One that is considered to be built with a hierarchy of twosomes. A binary morphological construction may be illustrated by the word *ungentlemanly,* in which the word is divided into two parts in succeeding steps down to its smallest individual parts:

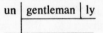

A binary syntactic construction is one in which word groups become successively smaller while undergoing this bipartite division:

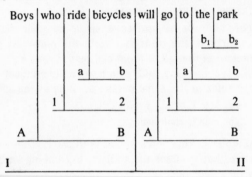

Many, though not all, English word groups can be divided into two constituent parts. (See IMMEDIATE CONSTITUENT.)

blending   A process of word formation in which, usually, the first part of one word is combined with the last part of another:

> *slip + glide = slide*
> *squeeze + crash = squash*
> *motor + hotel = motel*
> *smoke + fog = smog*
> *squall + squeak = squawk*

(See NONCE WORD.)

bound morpheme   One type of bound morpheme is that which can occur only with bases or stems. They are inflectional suffixes that have meanings such as "past tense," "plural," and "continuous action":

> burn*ed*   boy*s*   runn*ing*

or they are derivational suffixes:

> slow*ly*   advis*er*   act*ion*

or prefixes:

unkind   incapable   rehire

Some words contain two bound morphemes: a bound base and an affix:

tele|vise   hydro|phone

(See BASE, FREE FORM.)

breaking   A process, noted in the study of language history, in which vowels are diphthongized, or "broken" into two vowels. For example, in Old English the front vowels /æ ǣ : ɛ ɪ i:/ were "broken" by the effect of a following *h* or consonant cluster with *r* or *l*. These vowels became, respectively, the diphthongs /æə ǣ: ɛo ɪo io/. We can notice breaking in process in Modern English too. In the northern and western parts of the United States the historical vowels /e o/ are preserved, but they have become "broken," diphthongized, into two vowels in parts of the East Coast:

Northern	*Eastern*
/de/ "day"	/dei/
/et/ "eight"	/eit/
/se/ "say"	/sei/
/əgo/ "ago"	/əgou/
/kot/ "coat"	/kout/
/so/ "so"	/sou/

C

cant   A kind of slang used to exclude outsiders. It is the familiar, conversational language used and generally understood solely by members of a specified occupation, trade, profession, class, age group, or interest group. (See ARGOT, JARGON.)

case   In inflected languages like German, Old English, and Latin the nouns, pronouns, articles, and adjectives exhibit endings that signal nominative, accusative, genitive, and dative cases. These case endings are important in establishing grammatical relationships among words in a sentence. In English, a few case markers survive. The *-s* ending for plural and genitive (possessive) case of nouns is distinguished only in writing: boy*s*, boy'*s*. Otherwise, nouns have a common form: *boy*. The personal pronouns exhibit three cases: nominative, genitive, and, except for *it* and *you*, accusative: *I, my, me; he, his, him; we, our, us,* etc. (See ACCUSATIVE, DATIVE, GENITIVE, NOMINATIVE, VOCATIVE CASE.)

central vowel   A vowel articulated in the central part of the mouth. (See VOWEL.)

centum languages   These constitute one of the divisions of the Indo-European family of languages. The centum group is composed of the Tocharian, Hellenic, Italic, Celtic, and Germanic languages. In these languages the consonant /k/, as in Latin *c*entum, "hundred," was not palatalized to /s/ as it was in the satem language group. The /k/ remained as in Indo-European **kmtom,* Celtic *cant* or, in the Germanic group of languages, shifted to *h* in the First Consonant Shift: Old English *hund.* (See FIRST CONSONANT SHIFT, PROTO-INDO-EUROPEAN, SATEM LANGUAGES.)

checked vowel   A vowel followed by a voiceless consonant in the same syllable. English vowels are shorter — checked — before voiceless consonants than before voiced consonants: compare *seat* vs. *seed;* shorter when followed by /m n ŋ l/ + voiceless consonant than when a voiced consonant follows these four sounds: compare *rumple* vs. *rumble, seamstress* vs. *seam, kilt* vs. *killed.*

clause   *CG:* A sequence of words consisting of a subject and a predicate. An independent clause is a complete sentence; a dependent, or subordinate, clause is a word group that is part of a larger sentence. It is a word group that does not make complete sense standing alone, that depends for its completed meaning on one or more independent clauses. Dependent clauses can serve the grammatical functions of noun, adjective, adverb. *TG:* This term refers only to "relative clause" and "that-clause"; otherwise "sentence pattern" equates with the conventional meaning of *clause*. (See ADJECTIVE CLAUSE, ADVERB CLAUSE, INDEPENDENT CLAUSE, NOUN CLAUSE.)

clipping   A process of word formation in which the beginning or end of a word, or both, are cut off, leaving the part to stand for the whole. This remainder is called a clipped word: *lab, dorm, prof, pike* (road), *cello, Bert.* The clipping of the end of a noun is the most common process.

closed syllable   One that ends in a consonant. (See OPEN SYLLABLE, SYLLABLE.)

close(d) vowel   A high vowel, made with a relatively small opening of the mouth and the tongue raised toward the palate: oo /u/ is more closed than aw /ɔ/. (See HIGH VOWEL, VOWEL.)

cognate   Words related to each other by being descended from the same original word: German *essen:* English *eat;* Old Irish *brāthir:* English *brother.* The first two words are descended from Germanic **etan.* The second two come from Proto-Indo-European **bhrāter.*

collective noun   A noun whose singular form indicates a group of people, acts, things. Some common collective nouns are *army, contents, crowd, public,* etc. When a collective noun names the whole group, it agrees with a singular verb and a singular pronoun:

> The *flock* has found *its* place to graze.

When the noun names the individuals of the group it takes a plural verb and a plural pronoun:

> The *team have* found *their* uniforms.

The rules for using collective nouns are complicated because some of them have regular plural forms (*band/bands*) and some do not (*contents, mankind*). Further, some collectives habitually take singular verbs (*mankind, crowd*), while others more commonly take the plural verb form (*people*).

colloquial   Denoting a level of spoken and written usage. The level consists of familiar words and idioms used in informal speech and writing, but not considered formal enough for business correspondence or public speaking. (See USAGE.)

common noun   A noun that may refer in common to any or all the members of a group of persons, places, or things: *tree, dogs, magazine,* etc. (See PROPER NOUN.)

comparative degree   The comparative degree of a monosyllabic adjective or adverb ends in *-er* and is used when speaking or writing of two things:

Bill is fast*er* than Joe.
Bill runs fast*er* than Joe.

More indicates the comparative degree of polysyllabic adjectives and adverbs: *more important, more slowly.* (See COMPARISON, SUPERLATIVE DEGREE.)

comparison   Refers to adjectives and adverbs when they are used to indicate degrees of quantity, intensity, or superiority in quality. Three degrees of comparison are recognized: (1) the positive, which is indicated by the base form of the word: *fine;* (2) the comparative, which is indicated by *-er* added to the base: *finer;* (3) the superlative, which is indicated by *-est* added to the base: *finest. More* and *most* preceding polysyllabic adjectives and adverbs indicate comparative and superlative degrees, respectively: *more acrimonious, most acrimonious.* (See COMPARATIVE DEGREE, SUPERLATIVE DEGREE.)

compensatory lengthening   The lengthening of a vowel to compensate for the loss of a following consonant. In Old and Middle English *knight* is spelled *cniht* and *kniȝt* and pronounced with a voiceless velar fricative /x/ before *t*: /knɪxt/. When the velar fricative was lost in pronunciation, the vowel was lengthened and eventually became the diphthong: /nait/.

compensatory shortening   The shortening of a vowel when a consonant that follows it is doubled: Latin *lītera → littera.*

competence   *TG:* Describes what the speakers of a language are *competent* to produce rather than what they actually do produce. A transformational grammar can be described as a competence model since it describes a native speaker's abstract ability to produce an infinite number of different sentence structures and this speaker's ability to understand sentences that he has never heard before. (See TRANSFORMATIONAL GRAMMAR.)

complement   *CG:* A grammatical complement is usually thought of as (*a*) the direct object or (*b*) the indirect and direct object of a transitive verb. The complement of a linking verb is (*c*) a predicate adjective that modifies the subject or (*d*) a predicate noun that means the same thing as, is equivalent to the subject, and, like the predicate adjective, completes the meaning of the sentence.

(*a*) John eats *steak.*
(*b*) John gave *Bill a dog.*
(*c*) John felt *sick.*
(*d*) John is *chairman.*

A noun complement after linking verbs is also known as subject complement, the predicate nominative, and the predicate noun. *TG:* The optional noun complement position immediately follows an NP. It may be filled by an insert sentence transformed into a *that*-clause:

the car *that Joe drives*

Transformations that convert basic sentences into inserts to be embedded after NPs are called complementizer transformations. The *that* transformation illustrated above is one kind of complementizer transformation. (See COMPLEMENTIZER TRANSFORMATION.)

complementary distribution   The distribution of two similar items is complementary when they occupy different territories that do not overlap. Thus, the noun-plural morpheme $\{-s_2\}$ has among its allomorphs /s/ and /z/ which are in complementary distribution: /s/ follows voiceless sounds, /z/ follows voiced sounds.

complementary infinitive   *CG:* An infinitive that occurs in the verb complement position: I'm willing *to invite* her.

complementizer transformation   *TG:* A transformation that converts basic sentences into inserts to be embedded after NPs. There are three frequent kinds of complementizer transformations.

1. The *that complementizer* inserts *that* before an insert sentence that does not have an NP in common with the main sentence. This is different from the *relative that* transformation.

Main Clause Sentence: The car is wrecked.
Insert Sentence: Joe drives.
Transformation: The car *that Joe drives* is wrecked.

2. The *infinitive complementizer* inserts *for* before the first NP of an insert sentence and *to* after it.

Main Clause Sentence: There is something.
Insert Sentence: John reads.
Transformation: There is something *for John to read.*

3. The *gerunditive complementizer* attaches *'s* to the first NP of an insert sentence and *-ing* to the verb.

Main Clause Sentence: John completed his requirements.
Insert Sentence: John passed the examination.
Transformation: *John's passing* the examination completed his requirements.

Complementizer transformations also convert sentences into inserts to be embedded after verbs that take complements.

Main Clause Sentence: The man knows SOMETHING.
   Insert Sentence: The book is good ⇒ the book to be good.
   Transformation: The man knows *the book to be good.*

In the example above, the *infinitive nominal transformation* changes
the insert sentence so that it can fill the complement position marked
by the pro-form SOMETHING. The verb *know* can also take a *that*-clause
nominal (The man knows *that the book is good.*), a *wh-word* nominal
(The man knows *what* is good.) or a *verb-based noun* nominal (The man
knows *its avoidance of bad style.*). The verb *know* cannot take a *gerund
nominal* (*The man knows *its being good.*), but *prevent* can take a *ger-
und nominal* as its direct object (The man prevents *its being good.*).
Some other complement verbs are *expect, believe, try, want, find,
avoid, imagine,* etc. The conventional complements of transitive and
linking-type verbs are accounted for in the base rules of transformational grammar. These rules specify that complements follow the
verb:

$$MV \rightarrow \begin{Bmatrix} BE + pred \\ \ldots \ldots \end{Bmatrix} \quad \text{and} \quad V \rightarrow \begin{Bmatrix} V_{int} \\ V_{tr} \end{Bmatrix} + Nom \end{Bmatrix}$$

(See OBJECT COMPLEMENT, RULE OF GRAMMAR.)

complex sentence   *CG:* A sentence that consists of one independent
clause and any number of dependent clauses. The dependent clause
or clauses may occur before the independent clause at the beginning
of the sentence:

When I get home, I'll read to you.

after the independent clause:

I'll read to you *when I get home.*

or inside the independent clause. When it is inside the independent
clause, the dependent clause can serve as a modifier:

The man *who came to dinner* is my uncle.

as a subject:

Whoever wins the election confronts problems.

or as an object:

We know *what you are supposed to do.*

(See SUBORDINATION.)

complex transformation   *TG:* The process by which an insert sentence is embedded into a main-clause sentence.

The man knows S

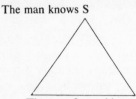

The man forgot his coat ⟹ that he forgot his coat

Readout: The man knows that he forgot his coat.

This is a general term for the process of forming complex sentences. (See MULTIPLE COMPLEX TRANSFORMATION, TRANSFORM.)

compound sentence   *CG:* A sentence that consists of at least two independent clauses joined by at least one coordinating conjunction or a semicolon: *John ran and Bill walked. John ran, Bill walked, but Sue rode her horse. John ran home; Bill walked.*

compound-complex sentence   *CG:* A sentence made up of two or more independent clauses and at least one dependent clause:

I don't know *what he wants* and I don't care.
      Dep. Clause

compound word   Words printed either as one word or hyphenated: *birdhouse, inside, father-in-law.* Morphemically, a compound word is a free form consisting of two or more free forms. Some compound words must be differentiated from grammatical constructions consisting of the same free forms. This is done by stress patterns. For example, the following contrasts are common in American English:

Compound Word	*Grammatical Construction*
bluebird	blue bird
greenhouse	green house
bull's-eye	bull's eye

(See STRESS.)

concatenation   *TG:* An operation that forms strings of symbols. This operation is symbolized by +. Thus, we have the free and bound morphemes *the, dog, s, ed, jump* which appear concatenated in this string of symbols:

the + dog + s + ed + jump

(See TERMINAL STRING.)

concord   Another word for AGREEMENT.

concrete noun   *CG:* Nouns that name persons, places, or things that can be perceived by the senses: *water, grass, tree,* etc. *TG:* Concreteness is a property of some nouns. The two subclasses of concrete nouns are *animate* and *inanimate* nouns. (See LEXICAL PROPERTIES.)

conditioning   See MORPHOLOGICAL CONDITIONING, PHONOLOGICAL CONDITIONING.

conjoining transformation   A simple transformation that joins two or more basic sentences with conjunctions such as *and, but, or, nor, either . . . or, neither . . . nor, both . . . and,* and *not only . . . but also.* For example:

> The plane took off *and* they all cheered.
> *Either* you take the exam *or* you fail the course.

conjugation   A conjugation represents a series of changes in a verb by means of prefixes, suffixes, or infixes. These changes represent such factors as person, number, tense, voice, mood. Here is a conjugation of the Old English strong verb *singan* "to sing."

	PRESENT			PRETERIT	
	Indicative			*Indicative*	
Singular	*Plural*		*Singular*	*Plural*	
1. singe	1. singað		1. sǫng	1. sungon	
2. singest	2. singað		2. sung	2. sungon	
3. singeð	3. singað		3. sǫng	3. sungon	

	Optative			*Optative*	
1–3. singe	1–3. singen		1–3. sunge	1–3. sungen	

	Imperative	
2. sing	2. singað	

Infinitive. singan
Gerund. tō singanne
Pres. Ppl. singende   *Past Ppl.* (ge)sungen

(See ACCIDENCE, INFLECTIONAL SUFFIX, PARADIGM.)

conjunction   A conjunction connects words, phrases, and clauses. (See CONJOINING TRANSFORMATION, COORDINATORS, CORRELATIVES, SUBORDINATION, SUBORDINATOR.)

conjunctive adverb   *CG:* A connective word or phrase used with adverbial force between independent clauses. This connects the first clause to a qualifying clause: "He writes forcefully; *however,* he needs to check his facts." Most common conjunctive adverbs, besides *however,* include *therefore, nevertheless, still, thus, yet, moreover, besides, consequently, as a result, on the other hand.*

consonant   A speech sound produced by some kind of an obstruction to the flow of breath. A momentary stoppage and then a release of the breath produces /p, t, k, b, d, g/. A stoppage at one place and then escape at another produces /m, n, ŋ, l/. Forcing the breath through a loosely closed or narrow passage produces /f, v, s, z, š, ž, θ, ð, h/. A stop plus friction produces /č, j/. /y, r, w/ are made by gliding the tongue between vowel sounds. Consonants are produced variously with and without the voice. The term consonant is also used rather loosely to mean a character in the alphabet that represents any of the above sounds or combinations of them.

consonant shift   See FIRST CONSONANT SHIFT.

constituent   Any word or construction that is part of a larger construction. Constituents of a phrase can be words, as in

>   the| boy

or constructions, as in the first two constituents of this sentence:

>   *The boy| walked home.*

The concept of constituents is useful in parsing sentence structure. (See IMMEDIATE CONSTITUENT.)

constituent sentence   See INSERT SENTENCE.

construction   A syntactic construction is any group of words that are knit together in grammatical relationships. A complete sentence is a construction, as are subordinate sentences and word groups with verbs, nouns, adjectives, and prepositions as their headwords. Morphological constructions are those which consist of a combination of free morphemes or of a free morpheme and one or more bound morphemes:

>   *fire|man   cat|s   un|tie   un|man|li|ness*

The concept of syntactic constructions is useful in analyzing the internal grammatical structure of the constituents of a sentence. (See HEADWORD, IMMEDIATE CONSTITUENT, SYNTACTIC CONSTRUCTION.)

consumer sentence   See MAIN-CLAUSE SENTENCE, MATRIX SENTENCE.

contact clauses   Two or more independent clauses written together to form a sentence without any connecting words between them are called contact clauses:

>   He came, he saw, he conquered.

continuant   A speech sound in which there is a continuous, uninterrupted flow of air. This classification includes vowels and some consonants. (See FRICATIVE, GLIDE, LATERAL, NASAL.)

contraction   The written form of words which indicate colloquial pronunciation by substituting an apostrophe for one or more letters of the standard spelling:

>   *hasn't: has not   he's: he is   won't: will not*

co-occurrence   The term describes a feature basic to linguistic structure. A number of grammatical relationships can be considered co-occurrence relationships, relationships that exist between two or more classes of words and/or constructions that occur in easily described positions in sentences.

The first kind of co-occurrence relationship is *simple dependence* between two or more classes. In this relationship, the occurrence of one class requires the occurrence of other(s), but not vice versa. For example, in sentences like

> He walked slowly.
> She walked in the garden.

the presence of an adverb or prepositional phrase in the predicate requires the presence of a verb, but the presence of a verb does not require the occurrence of an adverb or prepositional phrase:

> He walked.
> She walked.

The second kind of co-occurrence relationship is *mutual dependence* between two or more classes. In this relationship, one class always occurs with the other(s), and vice versa. For example, in sentences like *He walked. She walked.* the subject pronoun and the verb always co-occur. For these sentences to be grammatical, the occurrence of both of these classes is obligatory. In other words, the following are not English sentences: *walked, She.*

The third kind of co-occurrence relationship is a *mutually exclusive* one, either between two or more classes or between some members of one class and some members of another. For an example of the first type, in which the members of two or more classes can never co-occur in one position, observe that pronouns and nouns never co-occur in the subject position, nor do two pronouns or two nouns:

> *he Tom walks
> *he she walks
> *Tom Mary walks

For an example of the second kind of mutually exclusive co-occurrence relationship, in which some members of one class never co-occur with some members of another, observe that certain nouns cannot be the object of certain verbs:

> *The woman frightened the tree.
> *The man killed the gun.

(Adapted from A. Koutsoudas, *Writing Transformational Grammars* (New York: McGraw-Hill Book Co., 1966), pp. 95–96.)

coordinate clause   *CG:* Another name for INDEPENDENT CLAUSE.

coordination   Two or more words, phrases, or clauses that are equivalent in morphological or grammatical construction and are joined by a coordinating conjunction are said to be in coordination:

> running and jumping
> to run and to jump
> who were running and who were jumping

coordinators   Coordinating conjunctions, words that join items of equivalent grammatical construction; *and, but, for, nor, or, yet* are examples.

copulative verb   *TG:* These comprise one of the three large classes of English verbs, the other two being transitive and intransitive verbs. There are four subclasses of copulative verbs:

> (1) *Sense verbs: taste, smell, feel,* etc.
> (2) *Appearance verbs: appear, seem, look,* etc.
> (3) *Action verbs: grow, turn,* etc.
> (4) *Existential verbs: become, stay, remain.*

Sense verbs can be followed by adjectives:

> This beer *tastes* good.
> This plate *feels* cold.

These verbs have homophones that are transitive verbs and are thus followed by direct objects:

> John *tastes* the beer.
> He *feels* the pitcher.

In American English appearance verbs are not usually followed by nominals and, unlike sense verbs, they can take abstract nouns as subjects:

> His patriotism *seems* strong.

They can also be followed by the infinitive *to be:*

> He appears *to be* strong.

Action verbs can be followed by manner adverbs, whereas the previous two subclasses cannot be:

> He *turned* green slowly.
> Bill *grew* angry quickly.

Unlike most other copulative verbs, *become* can be followed by a nominal:

> Joe *became* president.

Like action verbs, *become* can also be followed by a manner adverb:

> Joe became president *unexpectedly.*

When *stay* and *remain* are used as copulative verbs, they share the characteristics of the verb *be*. They can be followed by nominals, adjectivals, and adverbs of location and time:

> Joe *stayed/remained* president.
> Joe *stayed/remained* happy.
> Joe *stayed/remained* in the bar.
> Joe *stayed/remained* in the bar for three days.

(See LINKING VERB.)

correlatives   Coordinators used in pairs. The most common are *both . . . and; either . . . or; neither . . . nor; not so . . . as; not only . . . but (also); whether . . . or.* (See CONJOINING TRANSFORMATION.)

count noun   A subclass of concrete nouns, count nouns have singular and plural forms and name objects that may be counted as separate units. They may be distinguished in their plural forms from mass nouns, which go with *how much: how much gold, how much coffee,* but not **how much dogs.* Count nouns in the plural go with *how many: how many dogs, how many boats,* but not **how many gold.* (An exception occurs in ELLIPSES: *How many red sunsets; how many gold?*) Count nouns generally do not stand alone in the singular, and can be preceded by the indefinite article in their singular form. (See MASS NOUN.)

counter-word   An automatic, often one-word response of like or dislike, acceptance or rejection. These words are usually overused, sometimes meaningless fad words creating a common bond of self-defense within a subgroup. Some slang counter-words for rejecting an outsider are *boob, creep, dope, drip, jerk, square.* For acceptance we can list words such as *gas, George, the greatest, nice, smooth, way out.*

creole language   One that has been expanded in grammar and vocabulary from a pidgin language from which it is immediately derived. Further, a creole language has speakers for whom it is a native language. It is not a dialect of any one of its parent languages since it is not mutually intelligible with other dialects of these parent languages. Examples of creole languages are the Creole French of Haiti and one of the coexistent varieties of English in Hawaii. (See PIDGIN LANGUAGE.)

cultural level of usage   Cultural levels of usage are based on the socioeconomic and educational background of the speakers of a language. There are generally two levels: *nonstandard* and *standard. Nonstandard cultural level* is identified by illiterate speech, ungrammatical speech and writing, excessive and unskillful slang, careless use of vocabulary. *Standard cultural level* is identified by cultivated language, clear, grammatical writing. Cultural level is to be contrasted with FUNCTIONAL VARIETY OF USAGE. Both of these concepts were formulated by John Kenyon. (See FUNCTIONAL VARIETY OF USAGE, USAGE.)

D

dangling modifier   *CG:* A modifier "dangles" when it is in a position to modify a word that it cannot logically modify. Dangling modifiers are most frequently participles. The subject of the main clause seems to be, but is not, the subject of the participle:

> Being only eight years old, his father drove him to school.

Infinitive phrases may be dangling modifiers:

> To run the mile, your stopwatch must be accurate.

So may prepositional phrases:

> At fifteen, his family took a long trip.

TG: A sentence modifier is derived, by transformation and embedment, from an insert sentence that has the same subject as a main-clause sentence.

Main-Clause Sentence:	John heard the storm.
Insert Sentence:	John was opening the door → opening the door
Readout:	Opening the door, John heard the storm.

Dangling modifiers result from two conditions. (1) When the insert sentence is ungrammatical:

Main-Clause Sentence:	The day was rainy.
Insert Sentence:	The day was looking out the window → looking out the window
Readout:	Looking out the window, the day was rainy.

(2) When two grammatical sentences are joined and give an illogical result:

Main-Clause Sentence:	Jane is an old grouch.
Insert Sentence:	Jane is a sweet girl → being a sweet girl
Readout:	Being a sweet girl, Jane is an old grouch.

(See EMBEDMENT.)

dative case   In inflected languages the dative case endings signal the indirect object. But English has no distinctive form for the dative case, thus it can hardly be said to have this case. In English, nouns that are indirect objects are in the common case form, and pronouns are in the objective case form. Thus, indirect objects in English are indicated by word order, the indirect object being the first of two nouns or noun equivalents after a transitive verb:

> He gave *Tom* the book.
> He gave *him* the book.

Or the indirect object is indicated by function words like *to* and *for*.

He gave the book *to Tom*.
He did it *for him*.

In *CG* the last two italicized phrases are called prepositional phrases.
(See CASE, PERIPHRASTIC CONSTRUCTION.)

declension   In inflected languages, the change in form of nouns, pronouns, and adjectives to show number, gender, and case. English nouns can hardly be said to have declension since they have only the genitive and plural inflected forms. There are variations in English pronouns, but they are irregular. Thus, Modern English does not have declension, at least in the sense that Latin and German have it. Old English, on the other hand, had many such inflections.

declarative sentence   One that conveys information; it makes a statement. (See MOOD.)

deep grammar   *TG:* The same as PHRASE STRUCTURE GRAMMAR. In this grammar the PHRASE STRUCTURE RULES operate.

deep structure   *TG:* These two sentences appear, at first glance, to be the same:

Lou is easy to please.
Lou is eager to please.

By "at first glance" we mean "on the surface." But notice how different they are when they are transformed into *It-Expletive* sentences:

It is easy to please Lou.
*It is eager to please Lou.

Superficially, these sentences are the same. Yet, they are different somehow. Linguists have posited that sentences have a *deep structure* and a *surface structure;* the two are related by transformations and by lexical rules. Further, deep structure may be the same as or different from surface structures. The deep structure of the simple, active, declarative sentence *He saw Suzie* is the same as its surface structure. On the other hand, the surface structure of the sentence *I know the girl who lives there* has a deep structure consisting of *I know the girl* and *The girl lives there*. Notice that the information implied in the structure *who lives there* is conveyed by the second deep structure sentence, *The girl lives there*. Thus it is said that the deep structure of a sentence contains its real meaning. In transformational grammar the deep structure of sentences is produced by the phrase-structure rules, which generate terminal strings, and by rules of affix transformation,

which change terminal strings into surface structures. (See INTERME-
DIATE STRUCTURE, SURFACE STRUCTURE, TERMINAL STRING.)

degree   See COMPARISON.

delayed subject   See **expletive.**

deletion transformation   A transformation that enables us to delete
words or phrases from sentences. The deletion transformation accounts
for shortened sentences in English. For example, when two kernel
sentences are joined to produce

> I like Joe and I like Lou.

a deletion transformation can remove the second *I like* to produce

> I like Joe and Lou.

The "short answer" is the result of a deletion transformation:

> *Question:*   Are you going to Denver?
> *Short Answer:*   Yes, I am.

Here, *going to Denver* is deleted to produce the "short answer."

demonstrative   This refers to the singular pronouns *this, that,* and
their plurals *these, those,* which indicate or point out.

dental consonant   This describes /d t n s/, sounds made by placing the
tongue tip against the back of the upper teeth. (See ALVEOLAR STOP,
FRICATIVE, NASAL)CONSONANT.)

dependent clause   *CG:* One that cannot stand alone and convey a
complete meaning. Dependent clauses are frequently introduced by
relative words and function as nouns:

> *That you like pie* is obvious.

as adjectives:

> The man *who likes pie* is here.

and as adverbs:

> I study *when I can find quiet.*

TG: Transformed insert sentences are dependent clauses. They are
introduced into main-clause sentences by an embedment transformation:

> *Main-Clause Sentence:*   SOMETHING is obvious. $\Big\}\Rightarrow$
> *Insert Sentence:*   You like pie $\Rightarrow$ That you like pie
> *Result Sentence:*   That you like pie is obvious.

Main-Clause Sentence:	The man (comp) is here.
Insert Sentence:	The man likes pie ⟹ Who likes pie
Result Sentence:	The man who likes pie is here.

⟹

Main-Clause Sentence:	I study SOMETIME.
Insert Sentence:	I can find quiet ⟹ When I can find quiet
Result Sentence:	I study when I can find quiet.

⟹

(See RELATIVE CLAUSE.)

derivation   The process of forming words from bases by adding one or more derivational suffixes or by changing one or more sounds. *Boyish, badly, reword, unbend* are derived by adding affixes (suffixes and prefixes). *Strength* and *deem* are derived from *strong* and *doom* by sound change in the vowel. (See ETYMOLOGY.) *TG:* The process of producing a basic sentence from the phrase-structure rules:

Phrase-Structure Rules	*Derivation*
$S \rightarrow NP + VP$	$NP + VP$
$VP \rightarrow Aux + MV$	$NP + Aux + MV$
$MV \rightarrow V$ (Adv)	$NP + Aux + V$ (Adv)
$V \rightarrow \left\{ \begin{array}{l} V_1 \\ V_{tr} + NP \\ V_C + Adj \end{array} \right\}$ (Adv)	$NP + Aux + V_{tr} + NP$ (Adv)
$NP \rightarrow (D) + N$	$(D) + N + Aux + V_{tr} + (D) + N$ (Adv)

Lexical Rules	*Application of Lexicon*
$D \rightarrow$ the, a	The $+ N + Aux + V_{tr} + a + N$ (Adv)
$N \rightarrow$ boy, ball	The $+$ boy $+ Aux + V_{tr} + a$ ball (Adv)
$Aux \rightarrow$ can	The $+$ boy $+$ can $+ V_{tr} + a$ ball (Adv)
$V_{tr} \rightarrow$ throw	The $+$ boy $+$ can $+$ throw $+ a +$ ball (Adv)
$Adv \rightarrow$ now	The $+$ boy $+$ can $+$ throw $+ a +$ ball (now)

(See LEXICON, RULE OF GRAMMAR.)

derivational suffix   In Modern English derivational suffixes include noninflectional endings that derive nouns from verbs (govern*ment*, play*er*), adjectives from nouns (use*ful*, act*ive*), and verbs from adjectives (social*ize*, sharp*en*). Derivational suffixes differ from inflectional suffixes in that (1) they do not end a word; inflectional suffixes can be added on after derivational suffixes (player*s*, sharpen*ing*); (2) derivational suffixes form words of a different class or new words of the same class. (See DERIVATION.)

descriptive grammar   As contrasted with prescriptive grammar, this grammar is concerned with describing the sounds, the word forms of, and the grammatical relationships within a language at a given stage in its development.

determiner   *SG:* Determiners are words like *a, an, one, this, that, any, no, some, their;* they pattern like *the.* These function words, and others like them, determine that sooner or later a noun will follow them.

> *the* man
> *a* big dog
> *that* gray stone house

TG: A determiner is either an ARTICLE like *the, a, that, this, these, those,* or a PRE-ARTICLE + an ARTICLE: *some of* + *the, all of* + *the, several of* + *the.* The base rule for determiners is

D → (PRE-ART) ART

(See POSTDETERMINER, PREDETERMINER.)

diachronic   Refers to a long period of historical time. Many linguists use the term as synonymous with "historical." (See SYNCHRONIC.)

diacritic, diacritical mark   A mark added to a letter or character to give it a particular phonetic value. In linguistics diacritics are used to indicate varying degrees of stress: ´ ^ ` ˘ . Other frequent diacritical marks are the dieresis (coöperate), and the cedilla (façade). (See STRESS.)

diagram   Systems of diagramming are used to represent, graphically, various structures encountered in the study of English syntax. There are three major conventions of diagramming:

Conventional Reed-Kellogg: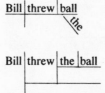

Structural: Bill | threw | the | ball

or the Chinese Box:

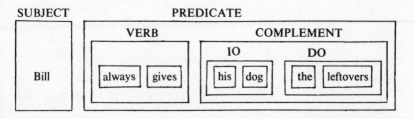

38   DIAGRAM

Transformational:

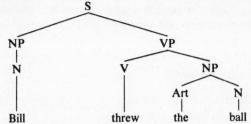

When we wish to represent an embedded sentence but are not interested in the details of its structure, we use a triangle:

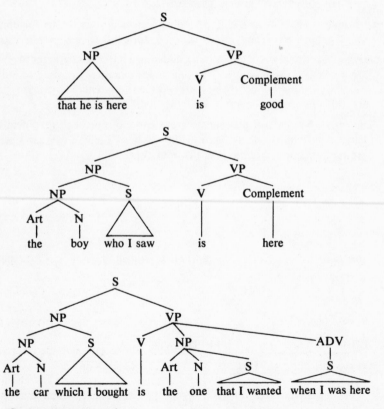

(See TREE DIAGRAM.)

REFERENCE: H. A. Gleason, *Linguistics and English Grammar* (New York: Holt, Rinehart and Winston, 1965), pp. 142–167.

dialect   Any one of the mutually comprehensible social or regional varieties of a language. Distinguishing features of a dialect are found in its pronounciation, grammar, and word-choice. (See MIDLAND DIALECT, REGIONAL DIALECT, SOCIAL DIALECT, PRESTIGE DIALECT.)

REFERENCES: H. B. Allen, and G. Underwood, *Readings in American Dialectology* (New York: Appleton-Century-Crofts, 1970); E. B. Atwood, *A Survey of Verb Forms of the Eastern United States* (Ann Arbor: University of Michigan Press, 1953); H. Kurath, *Word Geography of the Eastern United States* (Ann Arbor: University of Michigan Press, 1949); H. Kurath and Raven McDavid, *The Pronunciation of English in the Atlantic States* (Ann Arbor: University of Michigan Press, 1961); R. W. Shuy, *Discovering American Dialects* (Champaign: NCTE, 1967).

dialectology   The study of social and geographical dialects. (See DIALECT, LINGUISTICS, REGIONAL DIALECT, SOCIAL DIALECT.)

dictionary   The word list of a language. Although it is difficult to characterize all dictionaries since they vary in quality and kind, ten major items of information are usually found in a good, abridged desk dictionary:

1. *Main Entry:* The main entries follow one another in alphabetic order and are set in heavy black letters called **boldface type.**

2. *Pronunciation:* Pronunciations are shown by means of a system of phonetic transcription whose symbols are listed. Variant pronunciations are usually indicated.

3. *Function Labels:* Labels in *italics* indicate at least one of the eight parts of speech to which a given word belongs.

4. *Inflectional Forms:* Plurals of nouns, principal parts of verbs, and comparative and superlative forms of adjectives and adverbs are listed.

5. *Etymology:* The etymology traces an entry as far back as possible in English, tells what language a word came from into English, and traces the pre-English source as far back as possible.

6. *Vocabulary Entry:* The vocabulary entry defines and identifies a word.

7. *Status Labels:* Status labels indicate the temporal, stylistic, or regional status of a word.

8. *Usage Notes:* Usage notes, when they occur, provide information about the use of a word and, thus, further modify it.

9. *Cross References:* Cross references are of various kinds and serve to establish word relationships; they are usually given in SMALL CAPITAL letters.

10. *Synonyms:* Synonyms are generally found in a separate paragraph following the vocabulary entry.

TG: A dictionary is one of the two parts of the semantic component of a transformational grammar, the other part being projection rules, rules that show the relationship among dictionary meanings. This dictionary provides the meaning for each word in the sentence, for example, *dog:* its *syntactic properties* ("noun," "animate," "common," "count"); its *semantic properties* ("animal," "male," or "female"); its *phonological properties* in the form of distinctive features; its *distinguishers* ("a variable, carnivorous, domesticated mammal," "a worthless fellow," "a mechanical device for holding or fastening," "ruin"); and its selection restraints: the word *dog* has at least four meanings, each of which has certain restraints of selection on it. These allow the various readings to occur; (1) This dog is a good pet. (2) That man is a dog. (3) Tighten the dogs on the hatch. (4) Tom is going to the dogs. Selection restraints are, obviously, contextual features. (See DISTINCTIVE FEATURES, LEXICAL PROPERTIES, TRANSFORMATIONAL GRAMMAR.)

REFERENCES: P. B. Gove, *The Role of the Dictionary* (Indianapolis: Bobbs-Merrill, 1967); J. H. Sledd and W. R. Ebbitt, *Dictionaries and THAT Dictionary* (Chicago: Scott, Foresman, 1962); D. Starnes and G. E. Noyes, *The English Dictionary from Cawdrey to Johnson* (Austin: University of Texas Press, 1954).

digraph   A combination of two written letters representing one sound: *ph*one, *th*ing, *th*en, *pie*ce, *ea*t.

diphthong   A bundle of sounds connected by a tongue glide. The three phonemic diphthongs of American English are /au/, /ai/, /ɔi/ as in *cow, sigh,* and *boy,* respectively.

direct object   The person or thing receiving the action of the transitive verb. The direct object is the verbal, noun, pronoun, or noun clause following the verb:

> *Verbal:*   I like *swimming.*
> *Noun:*   I like *pie.*
> *Pronoun:*   I like *it.*
> *Noun Clause:*   I like *what he makes.*

discontinuous constituents   *SG:* Parts of the same grammatical construction whose continuous, common-order sequence is changed by the intrusion of other linguistic units:

The man *can walk : Can* the man *walk?*

dissimilation   A phonetic process in which two neighboring sounds that were once alike become different. In the words derived in English, Italian, and French from Latin *peregrinus* the first *r* has become dissimilar to the second one by changing to *l: pilgrim.* Sometimes one of the neighboring sounds will disappear completely. This kind of dissimilation is illustrated in the common pronunciations of *library, February, secretary* in which the first *r* is lost in each word.

distinctive features   Speech is heard as a chain of successive segments of sound. This auditory impression provides the linguist with an acoustic (contrasted with *articulatory*) basis for segmentation of sounds. It is on this acoustic basis that a good deal of phonetic analysis is now being done. Acoustic phonetics, a discipline based on the use of the Acoustic Spectograph which produces an exact visible record of speech, provides for a description of precisely what the ear hears. Speech sounds are described by their distinctive features, characteristics organized into bundles to form sounds. In this presentation of features we will consider each classification of sound variables as a set of binary, "yes/no," choices. Further, since an attempt has been made to greatly simplify the description, we will describe each feature on the basis of its acoustic or articulatory characteristics. In two instances we will resort to both bases for description. There are two large classes, and a number of subclasses, of distinctive features. One of the two main classes consists of *sonority features,* which are characterized by "the amount and concentration of energy in the [frequency] spectrum and in time." We will describe seven of the nine sonority features here. They are *Vocalic/Non-vocalic* Acoustic: the presence or absence of a sharply defined frequency differentiation. Vowels have a distinctive set of pitches. *Example:* /u/ vs. /k/. Articulatory: the mouth is open for vocalic sounds. *Consonantal/Non-consonantal* Articulatory: the presence or absence of an obstruction in the vocal tract. *Example:* /k/ vs. /l/. *Compact/Diffuse* Acoustic: a higher or lower concentration of energy in the central region of the frequency spectrum accompanied by an increase in the total amount of energy. *Example:* /ɛ/ vs. /ɪ/. *Nasal/ Oral* Articulatory: the oral resonance chamber supplemented by the nasal one versus exclusion of the nasal resonance chamber. *Example:* /m/ vs. /p/. *Tense/Lax* Articulatory: greater versus lesser tensing, deformation of the tongue muscles from their position of rest. *Example:* /ɪ/ vs. /æ/. *Interrupted/Continuant* Articulatory: the rapid turning on or off of sound either by closure-release or by one or more tongue taps versus absence of such an on-off mechanism. *Example:* /b/ and trilled /r/ vs. /l/. *Strident/Mellow* Acoustic: higher intensity noise versus lower intensity noise. *Example:* /s/ vs /θ/.

The other main class of features consists of *Tonality Features.* Here are two of the three. *Grave/Acute* Acoustic: predominance of the lower versus the upper end of the frequency spectrum. Articulatory: *Grave* consonants or vowels are pronounced with a larger, less-divided oral cavity; *Acute* consonants or vowels are pronounced with a smaller,

	p	b	m	f	v	k	g	t	d	θ	ð	n	s	z	č	ǰ	š	ž	ʊ	o	a	ɔ	ɪ	ɛ	æ	e
Vocalic / Non-vocalic	−	−	−	−	−	−	−	−	−	−	−	−	−	−	−	−	−	−	+	+	+	+	+	+	+	+
Consonant / Non-consonant	+	+	+	+	+	+	+	+	+	+	+	+	+	+	+	+	+	+	−	−	−	−	−	−	−	−
Compact / Diffuse	−	−	−	−	−	+	+	−	−	−	−	−	−	−	+	+	+	+	−	+	+	+	−	+	+	−
Grave / Acute	+	+	+	+	+	+	+	−	−	−	−	−	−	−					+	+	+	+	−	−	−	−
Flat / Plain																			+	+	−	+	−	−	−	−
Nasal / Oral	−	−	+	−	−	−	−	−	−	−	−	+	−	−	−	−	−	−	−	−	−	−	−	−	−	−
Tense / Lax	+	−	−	+	−	+	−	+	−	+	−		+	−	+	−	+	−								
Continuant / Interrupted	−	−		+	+	−	−	−	−	+	+		+	+	−	−	+	+	+	+	+	+	+	+	+	+
Strident / Mellow	−	−		+	+	−	−	−	−	−	−		+	+	+	+	+	+	−	−	−	−	−	−	−	−

Adapted from R. Jakobson, C. G. M. Fant, and M. Halle. *Preliminaries to Speech Analysis* (Cambridge, Mass.: MIT Acoustics Laboratory, 1952), p. 43.

(See ACOUSTIC PHONETICS.)

more divided cavity. *Grave* phonemes are back vowels and labial and velar consonants; *Acute* phonemes are front vowels and dental and palatal consonants. *Examples: Grave:* /m a/; *Acute:* /n ɪ/. *Flat/Plain* Articulatory: these features result from variations in lip-rounding or contraction of the pharyngeal tract: lip-rounding versus less rounding with concomitant increase in length of lip constriction; pharyngeal contraction versus less contraction. *Examples:* rounding: /ʊ/ vs. /ə/; contraction: /a/ vs. /æ/. This "yes/no" arrangement can be used to characterize the phoneme pattern of English.

do transformation   *TG:* A transformation associated with the yes/no question transformation. It is necessary to apply the do transformation when the tense affix is not followed by a verb or auxiliary word such as *have, be*, or by a modal auxiliary. The *do* form is added to carry tense. Here is an example:

Basic Sentence:	Bill -s- show his paintings.
Yes/No Question Transformation:	s- Bill show his paintings.
Do-Transformation:	Does Bill show his paintings?

The rule for the do-transformation can be written this way:

$$\left\{\begin{matrix} \varnothing \\ s \\ ed \end{matrix}\right\} \Big/ \begin{matrix} \text{in contexts other than} \\ + \text{ VERB, HAVE, BE,} \\ \text{MODAL} \end{matrix} \Big/ \Rightarrow \left\{\begin{matrix} \varnothing \\ s \\ ed \end{matrix}\right\} + \text{DO}$$

(See EMPHATIC ASPECT, NEGATIVE TRANSFORMATION.)

double-base transformation   *TG:* One of the names for a transformation that operates on two or more basic sentences:

Main-Clause Sentence:	Joe is a man (comp).
Insert Sentence:	Joe is old ⟹who is old ⟹
Result Sentence:	Joe is a man who is old.

(See COMPLEX TRANSFORMATION, DEPENDENT CLAUSE.)

double negative   The use of two negative words in the same statement to express a single negation:

I have*n't* got *none*.
She is *not* sure she *won't* be here.

doublet   One or the other of two words derived from the same source through different routes of transmission (for example, *cattle* and *chattel* derive from Latin *capitalis* via Middle English and Old French).

dual number   Identifies two persons, in contrast with singular (one) and plural (more than two), in the first- and second-person pronoun paradigms of Old English. The dual number pronouns of Old English are

	First Person		*Second Person*
Nom.	*wit* (we two)	Nom.	*git* (ye two)
Gen.	*uncer* (of us two)	Gen.	*incer* (of you two)
Dat.,		Dat.,	
Accus.	*unc* (us two)	Accus.	*inc* (you two)

These pronoun forms were used in Late Old English (tenth century) and Early Middle English (eleventh–twelfth centuries). All trace of the dual number was lost after the thirteenth century. (See PARADIGM, PRONOUN.)

E

ellipsis, elliptical construction   A construction in which an element existing in a related construction is missing:

> Are you going to Minneapolis? Yes, I am [going to Minneapolis].

(See DELETION TRANSFORMATION.)

embedment   A transformational operation in which an insert sentence is embedded into, added to, a main clause sentence. This transformation is the source of subordinate clauses and adverb and adjective modifiers in English. An example of embedment is given with the definition of DOUBLE-BASE TRANSFORMATION.

emphatic aspect   *CG:* The insertion of the verb *do* in a statement to put emphasis in the statement. The *do* verb then takes strong stress and indicates tense:

> He *does* drive.
> He *did* drive.

(See DO TRANSFORMATION.)

endocentric construction   A word group that functions in the same manner as its headword. *Old man* has a noun headword *man,* and the word group functions as a noun. *Very old* has an adjective headword *old,* and the word group functions as an adjective modifying a noun. (See EXOCENTRIC CONSTRUCTION, HEADWORD.)

epenthesis   An articulatory process by which an extra sound is inserted within a word, such as /p/ in *warmth, something* or /t/ in *sense.* The extra sound in the pronunciation is called excrescent. Most frequently after /m/ an excrescent /p/ may occur before voiceless consonants /t k f θ s š/. This process is further illustrated by the excrescent /p/ in *dreamt, comfort, Sampson.*

epithesis   An articulatory process by which an extra consonant is added to the end of a word. This extra consonant occurs after /s/ or /n/. After /s/, /t/ is added in some pronunciations of *once:* /wənst/, *across* /əkrɔst/. The word *midst* had the form *middes* in the fourteenth century. After /n/, /d/ is added. The words *bound* and *sound* were spelled *boun* and *soun* in the fourteenth century. (See ETYMOLOGY for the spellings of *sound.*)

eth   The written symbol ð, a modification of *d,* adopted in Old English times. It occurred within words and indicated both voiced and voiceless *th* sounds as in *thin* and *thine;* e.g., *oðer, cweðan.* (See THORN.)

etymology   The origin and development of the form of a word. The term also means the description of a word's etymology, tracing it back through history by means of historical and comparative linguistics. Here, as a sample, is the etymology of the word *sound* (the Roman numerals indicate the century of first recorded usage):

SOUND   (saund) that which is or may be heard, auditory effect. xiii (Cursor M.). ME. *sun, son, soun* — AN *sun, soun,* (O)F. *son* = Pr. *son, so,* Sp. *son,* Pg. *som,* It. *suono:* -L. *sonu-s* (whence also OE. *son,* ON. *sonn*). So *sound* vb. cause to make a sound xiii; emit a sound xiv. ME *sune, sone, soune* — AN. *suner,* OF. *soner* (mod. *sonner*) = Pr., Sp. *sonar,* Pg. *soar,* It. *sonare:* — L. *sonare,* f. *sonus.* ¶ The form with -d appears xv, and is established xvi.†

REFERENCE: C. T. Onions *et al., Oxford English Dictionary* (Oxford: Clarendon Press, 1933).

exocentric construction   A word group whose function is different from that of any of its constituents. *Bill sleeps* is neither a nominal expression like *Bill* nor a verbal expression like *sleeps*. In *to the house* the constituents are the preposition *to* and the noun phrase *the house,* yet the word group functions as an adverb of motion. (See ENDOCENTRIC CONSTRUCTION.)

excrescent sound   An INTRUSIVE CONSONANT.

expletive   In English the two expletive words are *it* and *there,* as they are used to get a sentence started. They have no explicit grammatical function in or connection with the rest of the sentence.

It is raining.
There is a man outside.

In the second construction *a man* is called the "delayed subject" because it comes after the verb with which it agrees. (See THERE TRANSFORMATION.)

eye dialect   A dialect perceived by the eye. It is a false phonetic respelling of common words to suggest nonstandard pronunciation. But it actually suggests the standard English pronunciation of many of the words it spells: *bekuz, nite, wuz, sez.*

†From C. T. Onions (ed.), *The Oxford Dictionary of English Etymology* (Oxford: The Oxford University Press, 1966), p. 848.

F

factive nominal   *TG:* A construction composed of *that + sentence,* which can be subject or object in certain kinds of sentences:

That he is honest is true.
I thought *that he would come home.*

factitive verbs   That small subclass of transitive verbs that make their two complements refer to the same person or thing. Factitive verbs are themselves of two classes: those that take two nominals as their complements

They *elected* Geoff president.
I *called* him an ape.
She *thought* him a fool.

and those that take a nominal and adjective as their complements:

He *painted* his house white.
I *consider* Eve good.

Factitive verbs are also called OBJECT COMPLEMENT verbs.

Family Tree Theory   A theory, characteristic of historical linguistics, in which a parent language such as Indo-European is regarded as having split into various different, yet related languages. The theory is useful in a general sort of way, and it has undergone considerable refinement in the last fifty years. The family tree diagram is a kind of gross representation of the theory. Here is a diagram suggesting the relationships among the various branches of Indo-European and the subdivisions of the Germanic branch.

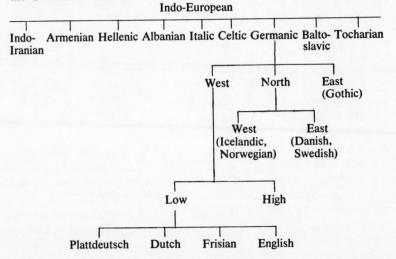

Indo-European

Indo-Iranian | Armenian | Hellenic | Albanian | Italic | Celtic | Germanic | Balto-slavic | Tocharian

Germanic:
West | North | East (Gothic)

North:
West (Icelandic, Norwegian) | East (Danish, Swedish)

West:
Low | High

Low:
Plattdeutsch | Dutch | Frisian | English

(See GLOTTOCHRONOLOGY, WAVE THEORY.)

REFERENCES: L. Bloomfield, *Language* (New York: Holt, Rinehart & Winston, 1933); Morton W. Bloomfield, "A Brief History of the English Language," in *The American Heritage Dictionary* (Boston: Houghton Mifflin, 1969).

Features of Words   See LEXICAL PROPERTIES.

finite verb   A verb limited in person by a pronoun or other subject nominal, in time by its tense form, or in number by the singularity or plurality of its subject. Finite verbs are contrasted with "nonfinite" forms of verbs, which are not limited in person or number: infinitives (*see, to see, to have seen*) and participles (*learning, learned*). The participle forms are also used as gerunds. Finite verbs are usually main verbs in sentences: *He runs. They ran.* Nonfinite verb forms combine with auxiliaries to form verb phrases that function as finite forms: He *was to have seen* it. They *had been learning.* (See NOMINAL.)

First (or Great) Consonant Shift   This was described by the German philologist Jacob Grimm in 1822. He observed a regular pattern of shift of certain Indo-European consonants in the Germanic languages. The Indo-European voiceless stops *p, t, k* became the Germanic voiceless fricatives *f, th, h.*

> *Example:*   I-E *p* = Latin *p* : L. *p*ater → Gmc. *f*ather
> I-E *t* = Latin *t* : L. *t*res   → Gmc. *th*ree
> I-E *k* = Latin *c* : L. *c*ent → Gmc. *h*undred

The Indo-European voiced stops *b, d, g* became the Germanic voiceless stops *p, t, k.*

> *Example:*   I-E *b* = Latin *b* : L. canna*b*is → Gmc. hem*p*
> I-E *d* = Latin *d* : L. *d*uo → Gmc. *t*wo
> I-E *g* = Latin *g* : L. *g*enus → Gmc. *k*in

The Indo-European voiced aspirated stops *bh, dh, gh* became the voiced stops *b, d, g.*

> *Example:*   I-E *bh* = Latin *f* : L. *f*rater   → Gmc. *b*rother
> I-E *dh* = Latin *f* : L. *f*oris   → Gmc. *d*oor
> I-E *gh* = Latin *h* : L. *h*ortus → Gmc. garden

Each of these sound changes took place only once. (See GRIMM'S LAW, INDO-EUROPEAN, VERNER'S LAW.)

flapped r   An allophone of /r/ in which the tongue tip momentarily touches the alveolar ridge once. It is heard in the British English pronunciation of *worry,* and in some dialects in the United States in which it sounds somewhat like /d/ or /t/. (See TRANSCRIPTION.)

focal area   An area whose economic, social, or cultural prestige has led to the spread of its linguistic forms into other areas. Focal areas in the eastern United States are Boston, Philadelphia, New York City, Richmond, and Charleston. The dialect features of focal areas are likely to have prestige when they are used by younger or more sophisticated speakers. (See DIALECT, RELIC AREA.)

folk etymology   The changing of the forms of words to fit what people think these words mean; the changing of the unfamiliar to the familiar by people who do not know the real etymology of a word. Words borrowed from other languages are particularly subject to the process of folk etymology. The Old French word *crévis/crévice* became Middle English *crevis(se)*, but has since been changed to *crayfish/crawfish* because the "meaningless" *-vis(se)* could easily be changed to the apparently similar native *-fish*. Other examples are Old French *primerole* → English *primerose;* Old French *mousseron* → English *mushroom.* Native words can also be altered in form and sometimes in meaning by folk etymology. *Hangnail* is derived from Old English *angnægl,* "tight or painful nail," in the sense of a growth like a corn in the foot. Now the form has been changed and the word is associated with fingernail. Other native folk etymologies include *bridegroom* from Old English *brȳdguma* "bride-man"; *hiccough* from earlier echoic forms such as *hickop, hicket.*

form class word   *Str:* A form class consists of words that share characteristic forms and pattern in the same ways in sentences. For example, nouns share the plural and possessive inflectional suffix *s,* a number of derivational suffixes such as *-er, -ment, -ness,* etc., and they pattern in generally similar ways with determiners, before and after verbs, and in constructions after prepositions. From the structural point of view, the four form classes are nouns, verbs, adjectives, and adverbs. There is some disagreement about pronouns, some of which show changes in form, some of which do not. (See FUNCTION WORD.)

fortis   When the stopped energy of the breath stream is great, the resulting stop consonant is a strong, or fortis, sound. Articulation and aspiration are usually stronger in the voiceless stops /p t k/ than in the voiced stops /b d g/. And these voiceless stops are, in English, fortis when they are in the initial position in a word. (See LENIS, STOP.)

free form   Free forms are bases and stems that carry lexical meaning and can stand alone: *boy, girlishness.* (See BOUND MORPHEME.)

free variation   Two sounds are said to be in free variation with each other when they can alternate in the same position in a word. Thus, /d/ and /t/ are in free variation with each other in the pronunciation of the past tense and past participle of the verb *burn:* burned/burnt. For some non-native speakers of English in Southeast Asia /s/ and /d/ are in free variation with each other in the pronunciation of the past tense of English verbs, both forms meaning the past tense: burne*d*/burn*s*. (See COMPLEMENTARY DISTRIBUTION.)

fricative   A consonant produced by friction caused by the air moving through a narrowed air passage in the mouth. Thus, audible friction is heard as the air is expelled. Fricatives are articulated at the meeting of the upper teeth and lower lip (voiced /v/, voiceless /f/); at the meeting of the tongue tip and the upper and lower teeth (voiced /ð/, voiceless /θ/; at the point of proximity of the tongue tip to the alveolar ridge (voiced /z/, voiceless /s/); at the point of proximity of the tongue tip to the palatal region just behind the alveolar ridge (voiced /ž/, voiceless /š/); and by the breath rushing through the vocal cords when they are constricted (voiceless /h/). (See CONTINUANT.)

fronting   A change in a vowel or consonant caused by moving the point of articulation further forward toward the front of the mouth. An example would be /u/ becoming /i/. (See UMLAUT.)

front vowel   A vowel articulated in the front of the mouth. These vowels are /i ɪ e ɛ æ /. (See VOWEL.)

functional shift   This term describes the ability of many words in English to be used, to function, as more than one part of speech. The manner in which a word is used in a given context determines its functional classification. Notice, for example, how *out* can be used in five different functions and can, consequently, be classified as five different parts of speech.

Noun:	He made the third *out*.
Adjective:	We saw only the *out*side of the house.
Adverb:	He ran *out*.
Part of two-word verb:	He dropped *out* of school.
Preposition:	He looked *out* the window.
	He was scared *out of* his skin.

functional variety of usage   Functional varieties of usage are based upon the function for which the usage is intended. John Kenyon posits two functional varieties of usage: *familiar-colloquial* and *formal-public*. The familiar-colloquial variety is identified by familiar conversation, private correspondence, informal conversation, and familiar public address. The formal-public variety is identified by pulpit or platform speech, public reading, worship, belles-lettres, and legal, scientific, or other expository prose writing. Martin Joos, in *The Five Clocks* (*International Journal of American Linguistics,* April 1962), discusses the "four usage-scales of native central English." These scales, all of which are influential in spoken and written usage, are Age, Style, Breadth, and Responsibility. Joos discusses five styles of usage: frozen, formal, consultative, casual, intimate. The frozen style is characteristic of print and declamation. It is characterized by the absence of authoritative intonation in the text and by the fact that the reader or hearer cannot cross-question the author. The purpose of formal style is to inform. It is characterized by the absence of participation on the part of the hearer and by the fact that neither the speaker nor the text is "involved"; the style is an objective one. The consultative, casual, and intimate styles are all characteristic of the colloquial mode. The consultative style is the norm for coming to terms with strangers. It is characterized by the fact that the speaker assumes no background information on the part of his listener; he supplies all this information. Further, the person who is addressed in this style is continuously participating in the discussion. The casual style is used with friends; it is the style for "insiders." This style uses ellipsis and slang. The intimate style is that used in an intimate group, usually between two people. It is characterized by the extraction of small units of wording or intonation from what in other situations would be longer lengths of discourse. These small units of wording or intonation are frequently a kind of code between two people. (See CULTURAL LEVEL OF USAGE, USAGE.)

function word   A term from structural grammar. Most function words, in their citation forms, have no lexical meaning. They lack inflectional forms and perform the syntactic function of connecting form-class words and sentences. The main function words are prepositions, conjunctions, determiners, auxiliary verbs, interrogative words, expletives, and some pronouns. (See FORM CLASS WORD.)

future tense   The tense that refers to time after the present. It is formed in the active voice by *shall*, more frequently *will*, plus the infinitive form of the verb:

> I shall go → I'll go.
> I will see → I'll see.

or by the present tense form of the verb plus an adverb:

> He graduates tomorrow.
> She goes next week.

Future time is also indicated by adverbials following verb phrases containing modal auxiliary verbs:

> We may leave soon.
> We must leave tomorrow.

and by adverbials following the uninflected form of the verb:

> We leave tomorrow.

Very frequently, the future is expressed by *going to:*

> I'm going to leave (tomorrow).
> We're going to leave (tomorrow).

future perfect tense   The tense that refers to a time after the simple present and before the simple future. It is formed in the active voice by *will* plus the infinitive form of *have* plus the past participle:

> will have turned
> will have gone

In the passive voice it is formed by *will* plus the infinitive of *have* plus the past participle of *be* and the main verb:

> will have been turned
> will have been gone

The future perfect tense is generally used in a context with the simple future:

> I will have gone by the time you will go.

and with the present:

> I will have gone by the time you go.

G

gemination   The process of lengthening or doubling, especially of consonant sounds. In West Germanic, for example, a single consonant other than *r* doubled (was geminated) when it was preceded by a short vowel and followed by *j*. Later the *j* changed the quality of some of the preceding vowels and finally disappeared. Thus, Germanic **cunja-* → W. Germanic **cunnja* → Old English *cynn;* Germanic **saljan* → W. Germanic **salljan* → Old English *sellan*. From the preceding examples it is obvious that gemination is indicated in writing by the doubling of a letter.

gender   English has what is called *natural gender*. The gender of nouns in English is masculine, feminine, or neither, according, literally and figuratively, to the sex or sexlessness inherent in the item the noun names. In English, then, gender is generally determined by the meaning of a word: *man, girl, rooster, hen, doe,* etc. The few exceptions to this statement are words that exhibit *grammatical gender*, a feature almost wholly lost in English by the fourteenth century. Pronouns such as *he, she, it* and a few nouns with feminine endings (*-ess, -ix, -euse*) and masculine endings (*-or, -us, -eur*) are the only remnants of grammatical gender in English. Grammatical gender is very much alive in inflected languages like French and German which have inflections for masculine, feminine, and neuter nouns and for articles and adjectives modifying them.

generative grammar   A term sometimes used to name transformational grammar, which actually consists of two parts: the generative and the transformational grammars. The generative grammar, while distinctly different from the transformational, is closely related to it. The generative grammar selects parts of speech and their subclasses on the bases of their co-occurrence and distinctive features, and puts them together to produce basic structures consisting of a NOUN PHRASE and a VERB PHRASE:

$$\frac{The\ man\quad walked\ home.}{NP\quad +\quad VP}$$

Basic structures are sometimes called deep structures. Transformations produce complex sentences from basic structures. (See CO-OCCURRENCE, DEEP STRUCTURE, KERNEL SENTENCE, TERMINAL STRING, TRANSFORMATIONAL GRAMMAR.)

genitive case   In its best-understood use, the genitive case indicates possession in English by the -'s/s' inflection on nouns, by the personal pronoun possessive forms *my, your, his, her, its, our, their*, and in part by the noun-replacive pronouns *mine, yours, hers, ours, theirs*. In many instances the genitive can be replaced by a prepositional phrase, usually with *of*, and sometimes by the uninflected form of a noun:

the report of the committee; the committee report
the cage of the bear; the bear cage

Besides representing possession, the genitive represents other relationships. (1) The *descriptive genitive* is evidenced in phrases such as *Chicago's new buildings, car's speed*. (2) The *subjective* and *objective genitive* occur with nouns naming an action. The subjective genitive is shown in *Joe's run* (Joe ran), *the scientist's discovery* (the scientist discovered). The objective genitive is illustrated by the *treasure's discovery* (someone discovered the treasure), *the robber's release* (someone released the robber). (3) Another genitive measures quality (*a dollar's worth*), space (*a stone's throw*), and time (*an hour's wait*). (4) The genitive of origin is illustrated by *Shakespeare's plays, duck's eggs*. (5) The partitive genitive establishes the relation of the part to the whole; this is expressed by of: *some of us, piece of pie*. (6) The appositive genitive employs *of*. It is sometimes used to show the relationship between two nouns or noun phrases that stand together, the second noun describing the first: *the state of Minnesota, the office of chairman*. (See CASE, POSSESSIVE INFLECTION.)

gerund   The verb form ending in *-ing;* when it is used as a noun, it is also called a verbal noun:

Swimming is fun.
I like *swimming*.
He did lots of *swimming*.

glide   In one sense, glide is the name for the phonemes /y r w/. In the second sense, a glide is a non-phonemic transitional sound made by the vocal organs in passing to or from the articulatory position for a speech sound. It is an *on-glide* if it precedes the sound [^{y}e]; it is an *off-glide* if it follows the sound [e^y]. (See CONTINUANT.)

glottal stop   This voiceless sound is the result of the compression and sudden release of air at the glottis. It is symbolized by /ʔ/. The glottal stop in English occurs initially before stressed vowels:

↓I run.

sometimes between vowels, when the second vowel begins a stressed syllable:

tri↓umphant

and sometimes as a transition from a final to an initial vowel:

India ↓ office

glottochronology   A statistical technique in which vocabulary similarities and differences permit deductions about the family relationship of languages as well as the probable dates when the branches of a given family separated from the common parent language. (See FAMILY TREE THEORY.)

REFERENCES: C. D. Chrétien, "The Mathematical Methods of Glottochronology," *Language,* 38 (1962): 11–37; S. C. Gudschinsky, "The ABC's of Lexicostatistics," *Word,* 12(1956): 175–210; M. Swadesh, "Lexicostatistic Dating of Prehistoric Ethnic Contacts," *Proceedings of the American Philosophical Society,* 96(1952): 452–63.

gradation   A change in vowel quality to one of the central vowels /ə ɨ ər/ when stress is reduced to weak stress. Consider these examples:

Strong Stress	Weak Stress	Gradation
John /ǽnd/ Jim	John /ən̆/ Jim	/æ/ – /ə/
He came /tú/	came /tə̆/ town	/u/ – /ə/
/əwé/	/ɔlwɨ̆z/	/e/ – /ɨ/
/fɔ́r/	/fər/ you	/ɔr/ – /ər/

(See ABLAUT.)

grammar   From the popular point of view the meaning of the term *grammar* is consonant with "correct usage," "linguistic etiquette." From the point of view of linguistics, grammar means the principles of operation of a language, or the study and description of these principles. When the structural linguist speaks of *grammar,* he means the morphology and syntax of a language. The transformational linguist describes *grammar* as a finite set of rules that generates an infinite number of grammatical sentences of a language, and no ungrammatical ones. This finite set of rules assigns to each sentence its correct structural description.

grammatical   In one of its meanings this word describes the morphological and syntactic portions, or "levels," of a structural grammar, the "grammatical level," as opposed to the "phonological level." The other sense of the term, "grammatical sentence," is very difficult to define. Clearly, this meaning has something to do with our intuitions about what is "structurally acceptable," but the various meanings of "intuition" and instances of "borderline" cases confuse the issue. *"The men is there" is clearly ungrammatical, but "The child seems sleeping" seems to be a borderline case.

grammatical meaning   That meaning which is conveyed by contrasting differences in word forms and grammatical structures. For example, the difference between *runs* and *ran* is the difference between the third-person singular present tense and the common form of the past tense. This term is contrasted with LEXICAL MEANING.

grapheme   Generally, any one of the written or printed alphabetic characters of a language. As a phoneme is a family of allophones and a

morpheme is a family of allomorphs, so a grapheme is a family of
ALLOGRAPHS, different shapes of the same letter. Thus A, a, *a*, and *A*
are four different allographs of the same grapheme which is written as
⟨a⟩. There are thirty-seven segmental graphemes of standard English
writing or printing. They are classified in two groups:

    (1) Twenty-six LETTERS OF THE ALPHABET: ⟨a, b, c, d . . . z⟩
    (2) Eleven PUNCTUATION MARKS: ⟨, ; : . ? ! ' " - – ( )⟩

Members of the series a b c d . . . z are called LOWER CASE. Members
of the series A, B, C, D . . . Z are called CAPITALS. Space can also be
included as a sort of zero grapheme since it is what bounds written
words on either side, thus defining them for most literate people.
Adapted from W. Nelson Francis, *The Structure of American English*
(New York: The Ronald Press Co., 1958), pp. 436–437.

REFERENCES: I. J. Gelb, *The Study of Writing* (Chicago: University of Chicago
Press, 1952); R. A. Hall, Jr., *Sound and Spelling in English* (Philadelphia:
Chilton, 1961).

Grassman's Law   Grassman's Law is a phonetic statement to the
effect that when two related languages have aspirated stops at the
beginning of two successive syllables, the first of the two stops becomes unaspirated in the later of the two languages.

pre-Greek	*Greek*
*[phewthomai]	[pewthomai]
*[thithe:mi]	[tithe:mi]
*[thrikha]	[trikha]

Great Vowel Shift   The change in pronunciation of accented long
vowel sounds that took place from the late Middle English period
(1400) until about 1750. The following chart describes these changes,
showing a written representation of these sounds at two periods and a
phonemic representation at three periods in the history of the English
language. See VOWEL for a description of the vowel phonemes and the
ways in which they are represented by phonemic transcription.

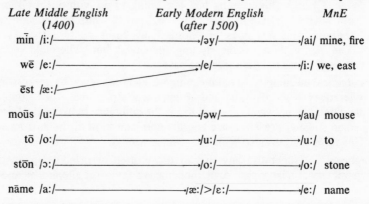

Late Middle English (1400)	Early Modern English (after 1500)	MnE
mīn /i:/	/əy/	/ai/ mine, fire
wē /e:/	/e/	/i:/ we, east
ēst /æ:/		
moūs /u:/	/əw/	/au/ mouse
tō /o:/	/u:/	/u:/ to
stōn /ɔ:/	/o:/	/o:/ stone
nāme /a:/	/æ:/>/ɛ:/	/e:/ name

Grimm's Law   The description of the shift in pronunciation in the Germanic languages of nine Indo-European consonants. (See FIRST CONSONANT SHIFT.)

H

headword   The word that is grammatically central in a construction because all other words in the construction modify it.

Noun Headword:	my old *friend; friend* of mine
Verb Headword:	sometimes quietly *talked; arrived* noisily yesterday
Adjective Headword:	exceedingly *cold; good* for nothing
Adverb Headword:	rather *slowly,* sometimes *outside;* a yard *away; away* for a month

(See ATTRIBUTE, CONSTRUCTION, NOUN-HEADED CONSTRUCTION, VERB-HEADED CONSTRUCTION.)

helping verbs   See AUXILIARY VERB.

high vowel   The vowel produced with the tongue raised toward the roof of the mouth. (See CLOSED VOWEL, VOWEL.)

homonym, homophone   These terms describe a word that is identical in pronunciation with another word whose meaning is different. Examples are *plain-plane; beet-beat.*

human noun   *TG:* Human nouns are a subclass of animate nouns that can co-occur with the pronouns *who/whom:*

who is the *boy*
man whom I saw

(See LEXICAL PROPERTIES.)

I

ideogram, ideograph   A symbol or group of symbols representing a word or phrase, but not representing the phonemes of the word or phrase. Examples from our own alphabetic writing are *5, +, $*. (See PICTOGRAM.)

idiolect   An individual's characteristic way of using his language as manifested in his pronunciation, grammar, and word-choice.

immediate constituent   The two parts into which every word group can be divided. These parts are constituent because they constitute the word group, and they are immediate because they are directly related to one another. ICs may be word groups

The boys│played yesterday

or single words

the│boys

For a description of the morphemic ICs, the immediate constituents of words, see the definition of CONSTRUCTION.

REFERENCE: C. C. Fries, *The Structure of English* (New York: Harcourt, Brace & World, 1952).

imperative mood   The mood of the verb used in giving a command or making a request. Normally, there is no subject of the verb in this construction:

Close the door.
Go away.

TG: The prevailing school grammar description of this sentence type still speaks of the "understood subject *you*." While this is not a precise description of this construction, there is an important, intuitive perception of grammatical process underlying it. Transformational rules should probably derive the imperative from a related sentence containing the modal auxiliary verb *will* so that we can account for imperative sentences such as

Close the door, will you?

The imperative transformation, then, might operate, first, by deleting *will*, then the subject *you*, from the basic sentence:

You will open the window ⟹You open the window ⟹Open the window.

It can now be seen that "understood subject *you*" can be interpreted as the result of an automatic deletion transformation. (See DELETION TRANSFORMATION.)

imperfect aspect   *CG:* The imperfect or durative aspect is frequently termed the imperfect tense. The imperfect notes an action or state of being that is still in progress in reference to some point in time, particularly the past. It is expressed in a number of ways in English. Among them are the progressive:

He is/was running.

the present or past form of the verb plus present participle as predicate:

He continues/continued running.

or by the addition of *on* or *on and on:*

He walked on alone.
He went on and on.

(See PROGRESSIVE TENSE.)

inanimate noun   *TG:* Inanimate nouns are a subclass of count nouns. They are those nouns that refer to inanimate objects and that can occur only as the subjects, not objects, of verbs like *surprise, frighten,* and *confuse:*

The *house* surprised the man.
The *mountain* frightened the explorer.
The *puzzle* confused Norman.

House, mountain, and *puzzle* refer to inanimate objects and cannot occur as objects of these verbs. (See LEXICAL PROPERTIES.)

indefinite pronouns   Pronouns that do not indicate one particular person or thing but, rather, any one or more of a class or persons or things. They have no explicit antecedent. *All, any, each, some, everyone, few, nobody,* and *you* and *we* in some of their uses are indefinite pronouns.

independent clause   A clause that can stand alone and convey a complete meaning. Independent clauses may be complete sentences:

The man is here.

or parts of sentences:

The man is here because he came home.

(See DEPENDENT CLAUSE.)

indicative mood   The mood of the verb that expresses a statement of fact. (See IMPERATIVE MOOD, INTERROGATIVE MOOD.)

indirect object   With verbs of giving, telling, etc., there is frequently an object that names the receiver of the thing or message. This indirect object is the first of two nominals after a transitive verb:

> I gave *the man* a dollar.
> He told *me* a story.

(See DATIVE CASE, PERIPHRASTIC CONSTRUCTION.)

indirect question   A question in which its substance, but not its exact words, is stated. The question clause is introduced by an interrogative word:

> I wonder *whether he has the car.*
> He asked *if they saw the fire.*

indirect statement   A quotation summarized or paraphrased in the writer's own words rather than being quoted as it was originally stated or written:

> He said that he wouldn't arrive until tomorrow.

Indo-European   The term describes languages belonging to the large group of related languages of which English is a member. The abbreviation is IE. (See PROTO-INDO-EUROPEAN, FAMILY TREE THEORY.)
REFERENCES: L. Bloomfield, *Language* (New York: Holt, Rinehart & Winston, 1933); S. Robertson and F. G. Cassidy, *The Development of Modern English* (Englewood Cliffs: Prentice-Hall, 1954).

infinitive   The infinitive is the stem form of the verb which is not limited in tense, person, mood, or number. *Run* is an infinitive. The form of the infinitive preceded by *to, to run,* is called the *marked infinitive*.

infinitive phrase   *To* plus the verb stem is also called the infinitive phrase. Infinitive phrases function as nouns:

> He tried *to go.*
> *To drive* is his idea of fun.

as adjectives:

> John has time *to think.*

and as adverbs:

> He's going home *to see* his parents.

infix   An inflectional or derivational affix inserted within a word rather than at its end or beginning. In English, infixes can indicate past tense (st*oo*d, h*u*ng) or plural (m*e*n, g*ee*se).

inflection   The same as an INFLECTIONAL SUFFIX and some INFIXES.

inflectional language   An inflectional language, also known as a SYNTHETIC LANGUAGE, is one in which the relationships among words, thus their functions, depend mainly upon inflections. For example, the Latin sentence *Agricola amat puellam* has the same meaning — "The farmer loves the girl" — no matter what the order of words is. The *-a* ending on *agricola* and the *-am* ending on *puellam* designate, respectively, the subjective (nominative) and objective (accusative) functions. Changing the word order makes no difference in meaning, as long as the endings remain the same; *Agricola puellam amat* still means "The farmer loves the girl." In Modern English, an ANALYTIC LANGUAGE, a change in the order of words makes a difference in meaning: *The farmer loves the girl : The girl loves the farmer.* Old English, like Latin and Modern German, was synthetic in its grammatical structure. (See ANALYTIC LANGUAGE, SYNTHETIC LANGUAGE.)

inflectional suffix   Affixes that occur with the stems of form-class words. They show number and possession in nouns:

> *Noun Plural:*   dog*s*, cat*s*, wom*e*n
> *Possession:*   boy'*s*, girl'*s*

number and tense and person in verbs:

> *3rd Singular Present Tense:*   she shop*s*, it burn*s*
> *Past Tense:*   shopp*ed*, burn*ed*
> *Present Continuous Tense:*   shopp*ing*, burn*ing*

and comparative and superlative degrees in adjectives and adverbs:

> *Comparative:*   slow*er*
> *Superlative:*   slow*est*

insert sentence   *TG:* A basic sentence that is embedded, introduced, into a main clause sentence by processes of transformation:

> *Main-Clause Sentence:*   Joe is a man (COMP) ⎫ ⟹
> *Insert Sentence:*   Joe is old ⟹ who is old ⎭
> *Result Sentence:*   Joe is a man who is old.
> *Deletion Transformation:*   Joe is a man who is old.
> *Adjective Rearrangement:*   Joe is an old man.

(See ADJECTIVE.)

intensifier   See QUALIFIER.

intensive pronoun   See PRONOUN.

intermediate structure   *TG:* A structure intermediate between a deep structure and a surface structure; it is a tree representing a deep structure on the way to being transformed into a surface structure. The following example shows an intermediate structure in which a sentence, on the way to becoming a relative clause, is being embedded after an NP, *the dog.* Notice that a relative word, *that,* has been substituted for a determiner, *the,* as part of the transformation.

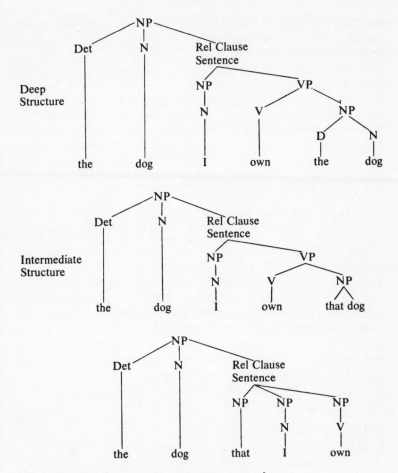

(See DEEP STRUCTURE, SURFACE STRUCTURE.)

International Phonetic Alphabet   See TRANSCRIPTION.

interrogative mood   The mood of the verb that expresses a question. (See QUESTION for the forms that express the interrogative mood.)

interrogative pronoun   Pronouns used to ask questions. They are *who, whom, whose, what, which.* (See INTERROGATIVE WORD.)

interrogative sentence   See QUESTION.

interrogative word   A term that designates a broader class of interrogators than just pronouns. Sometimes they are called *wh-words.* Interrogative words ask questions: *who, whom, whose, what, when, where, why, which, how,* etc. (See WH-QUESTION.)

intervocalic   Literally, "between vowels." Consonants and groups of consonants are intervocalic: me*t*er, chil*dr*en.

intonation Loosely, "way of talking." Linguists use the term to indicate distinctive speech patterns. (See INTONATION CONTOUR.)

intonation contour The intonation contours of English are phonemic combinations of pitch and terminal juncture that characterize various kinds of utterances:

Statement:	²He has a ³cold¹ ↓
	The intonation contour is 231 ↓
Yes/No Question in Statement Form:	²He has a ³cold³ ↑
	The intonation contour is 233 ↑
Wh-Question:	²Who ³is it¹ ↓
	The intonation contour is 231 ↓

(See PITCH LEVELS, SUPRASEGMENTAL PHONEME, TERMINAL JUNCTURE.)

REFERENCES: K. L. Pike, *The Intonation of American English* (Ann Arbor: University of Michigan Press, 1944); J. H. Sledd, *A Short Introduction to English Grammar* (Chicago: Scott, Foresman, 1959); N. C. Stageberg, *An Introductory English Grammar* (New York: Holt, Rinehart & Winston, 1965).

intransitive verb *CG:* A verb that does not take an object. *Go, sleep, look, laugh* are intransitive verbs. Many verbs may be used either intransitively or transitively. *Str:* Intransitive verbs cannot take an object in the active voice. Thus, they are complete predicates in themselves. They usually have no passive voice form. Intransitive verbs are words like *run, stop, sink, rise, lie, appear,* etc. *TG:* Intransitive verbs can be divided into three subclasses: (1) verbs like *sleep,* which may have no post-verbal element; (2) verbs like *sit,* which usually select adverbs of location after them; (3) verbs like *run,* which may select adverbs of motion after them (He *ran into the house*). In certain circumstances intransitive verbs require either adverbs of motion or adverbs of location, but not both. The expansion rule for intransitive verbs attempts to show such restriction. (C) allows for the optional development of an additional element in the complement:

$$V_{int} \longrightarrow \left\{ \begin{matrix} V_i \\ \begin{bmatrix} V_{iL} + \text{LOC} \\ V_{iM} + \text{MOT} \end{bmatrix} \quad (C) \end{matrix} \right\}$$

intrusive consonant A consonant that comes into a word as a result of the process of articulation; this consonant is not found in the etymology of the word. The intrusive *r,* found in the speech of many "r-less" areas of the United States, particularly in the east, occurs most often after /ə/ and links one word with another: *lawr office, idear of, sawr a girl.* Intrusive *d* and *t* occur after *n* and before *s.* As the tongue moves from the alveolar position of /n/ to the open position of /s/ it releases air, producing an excrescent /d/ or /t/. Compare your pronunciations of *bands : bans, finds : fins* and *cents : sense, prints : prince* to hear these excrescent sounds. (See ARTICULATORY INTRUSION, EPENTHESIS, EPITHESIS.)

inversion   Grammatical inversion consists of placing a verb before the subject as in the question pattern *Are you going?* or *Did he go?* Inverted word order was a common feature of declarative sentences in the early stages of the development of the English language:

> *Old English:*   þā cwǣdon þā cristenan, "then said the Christians"
> *Middle English:*   Speke we now of wikked conseil

irregular verb   Irregular verbs in English are in contrast with regular verbs, which form their past tense and past participle by adding *-ed* to the infinitive. Irregular verbs, the "strong verbs" of Old English, form their past tense and past participle through change in the root vowel:

Infinitive	*Past Tense*	*Past Participle*
fall	fell	fallen
lie	lay	lain
ride	rode	ridden
see	saw	seen
spring	sprang	sprung

isogloss   A line on a dialect map connecting points at which a specific feature of pronunciation, grammar, or vocabulary exists. A number of isoglosses that generally delineate the same area is considered to be a dialect boundary. Where the dialectologist finds that one pronunciation or word is used almost entirely in one area, he draws a line, an isogloss, which marks the boundary of the use of that item. The map below shows the isoglosses marking the distribution of *frijoles* (pinto beans) and *pilón* (something extra) in Texas:

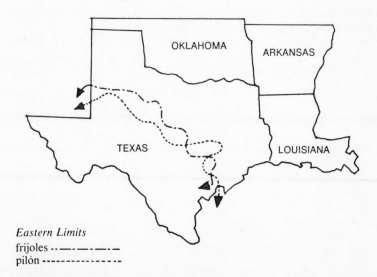

Eastern Limits
frijoles ··—··—··—··—
pilón ····················

From E. Bagby Atwood, *The Regional Vocabulary of Texas* (Austin: University of Texas Press, 1962), map 116, p. 246.

REFERENCE: H. B. Allen, "The Primary Dialect Areas of the Upper Midwest," in H. B. Allen (ed.), *Readings in Applied English Linguistics*, rev. ed. (New York: Appleton-Century-Crofts, 1964).

isolating language   A language like Chinese that consists of invariable, usually monosyllabic, root words. The relation between words is expressed by word order or by variations in tonal pattern. An isolating language is similar to an ANALYTICAL LANGUAGE.

J

jargon   The technical "shop talk" or, in some instances, the secret vocabulary of a specific occupation, trade, profession, class, age group, etc. (See ARGOT, CANT.)

juncture   A feature of spoken utterances that describes the various kinds of transitions of pitch and pause within a complete utterance and between utterances. (See SUPRASEGMENTAL PHONEME, TERMINAL JUNCTURE.)

kernel sentence   *TG:* The kernel, or basic, sentence is simple, active, declarative, affirmative. Kernel sentences are generated by phrase structure rules and by obligatory simple transformations. They are the sentences upon which optional simple and complex transformations operate.   (See GENERATIVE GRAMMAR, SIMPLE TRANSFORMATION.)

L

labeled-tree diagram   See TREE DIAGRAM.

labial consonant   Consonants in whose formation the lips play the important functions of stopping or stopping and releasing the flow of air. /b p m/ are labial consonants.

labio-dental consonant   These are made by friction of the air passing through a point at which one lip is in contact with the cutting edge of the teeth. /v f/ are labio-dental consonants.

language   A system of arbitrarily chosen vocal sounds by which a group of people communicate with one another. Some languages have a roughly or closely corresponding set of arbitrarily chosen symbols that constitute a writing system. Natural languages, then, are those thousands of systems of vocal sounds that have developed in the course of human history. The term *language* is also applied to artifical systems such as Esperanto, to systems of written or printed symbols such as Fortran IV (a computer "language"), to systems of communication used by animals and insects, and to systems such as signs and colors in various media.

langue   A concept of the Swiss linguist Saussure (1857–1913). It is that part of the system of language which is inherited; it is the complete grammatical system used by the speakers of a language. It is contrasted with PAROLE, an individual speaker's utterance of the language. (See COMPETENCE, PAROLE.)

REFERENCE: F. Saussure, *A Course in General Linguistics*, Wade Baskin, trans. (New York: McGraw-Hill, 1966).

lateral sound   A consonant sound produced by the air flowing laterally off one or both sides of the tongue. The tip of the tongue is pressed against the alveolar ridge to stop the flow of air. /l/ is a lateral. (See CONTINUANT.)

lax vowel   A vowel articulated with relatively little tension of the tongue muscles. Compare the lax vowels /ɪ/ and /ɛ/ against the tense vowels /i/ and /e/.

lenis   When the stopped energy of the breath stream is relatively slight, the resulting stop consonant is a weak, or lenis, sound. Articulation and aspiration are usually weaker in the voiced stops /b d g/ than in the voiceless stops /p t k/. (See FORTIS, STOP.)

leveling of inflections   A process that takes place as a result of NEUTRALIZATION and ANALOGY. In Old English one of the vocalic declension noun classes had the following inflectional endings:

MASCULINE	NEUTER
Singular	

MASCULINE	NEUTER
-	-
es	es
e	e

Plural

MASCULINE	NEUTER
as	u
a	a
um	um

In Middle English these endings are leveled to:

Singular	*Plural*
-	es
es	es
(e)	es

In Modern English further leveling has taken place:

Singular	*Plural*
-	s
-	s
-	s

(See ANALOGY, NEUTRALIZATION.)

REFERENCE: S. Robertson and F. G. Cassidy, *The Development of Modern English* (Englewood Cliffs: Prentice-Hall, 1954).

levels of usage   See CULTURAL LEVEL OF USAGE, USAGE.

lexeme   A meaningful speech form, a word or a stem. It is an item in the vocabulary of a language.

lexical meaning   English nouns, verbs, adjectives, and adverbs have lexical meaning,—a meaning that can be found in a dictionary. These four classes of words can be contrasted with FUNCTION WORDS, most of which have no meaning until they connect words in a sentence. (See GRAMMATICAL MEANING.)

lexical properties   *TG:* Every speaker of English has an innate knowledge of the properties of words, a kind of internalized dictionary that determines the ways in which words go together in the DEEP STRUCTURE of sentences. This internalized dictionary is part of the lexical entry in the LEXICON, or DICTIONARY, of a TRANSFORMATIONAL GRAMMAR. The properties of words in the lexicon are represented as sets of features. The presence of a feature is shown by a plus (+) sign, the absence of a feature by a minus (−) sign. NOUNS have many different properties. They may be *common* ("boy") or *proper* ("Joe"). Common nouns have the feature ⟨+common⟩; proper nouns have the feature ⟨−common⟩. Common nouns are either *concrete* ("tree") or *abstract* ("luck"). Concrete nouns have the feature ⟨+concrete⟩; abstract nouns have the feature ⟨−concrete⟩. Concrete nouns are either *animate* ("puppy") or *inanimate* ("mountain"). Animate nouns show the feature ⟨+animate⟩; inanimate nouns show the feature ⟨−animate⟩. Animate nouns are either *human* ("girl") or *nonhuman* ("horse"). Human nouns and nonhuman nouns show the features ⟨+human⟩ and ⟨−human⟩. The noun *man* is listed in the lexicon like this:

$$
\text{man}
\begin{bmatrix}
+N \\
+\text{common} \\
+\text{concrete} \\
+\text{animate} \\
+\text{human}
\end{bmatrix}
$$

The entry for *luck* looks like this:

$$
\text{luck}
\begin{bmatrix}
+N \\
+\text{common} \\
-\text{concrete} \\
-\text{animate} \\
-\text{human}
\end{bmatrix}
$$

These features can be an important influence in the choice and arrangement of words in the deep structure of sentences. In the following sentences, for example, the distinction between ⟨+animate⟩ and ⟨−animate⟩ explains part of the ungrammaticality of the starred sentence:

The mountain frightened the man.
*The man frightened the mountain.

$$
\begin{bmatrix}
\langle+\text{common}\rangle \\
\langle+\text{concrete}\rangle \\
\langle+\text{animate}\rangle
\end{bmatrix}
\qquad
\begin{bmatrix}
\langle+\text{common}\rangle \\
\langle+\text{concrete}\rangle \\
\langle-\text{animate}\rangle
\end{bmatrix}
$$

Some noun features can be ⟨+⟩ or ⟨−⟩ for the same word, depending on its syntactic environment. Most English nouns can be *singular* (⟨+singular⟩) or *plural* (⟨−singular⟩) in the same sentence:

The boy likes to run.
The boys like to run.

But some nouns like *gold* and *dirt* can be only ⟨+singular⟩. Nouns can also be *definite* (⟨+definite⟩) or *indefinite* (⟨−definite⟩) depending on whether they are preceded by the definite article *the* in the singular and plural or by the indefinite articles *a, an* in the singular or by no article at all in the indefinite plural. Personal PRONOUNS have features of number, person, gender, and case. These features can be summarized in this way:

Number	Person and Gender	Case
$\langle$+singular$\rangle$	$\langle$+I$\rangle$	$\langle$+accusative$\rangle$ *me*
		$\langle$−accusative$\rangle$ *I*
	$\langle$+II$\rangle$ *you*	
	$\langle$+III$\rangle$ $\langle$+male$\rangle$	$\langle$+accusative$\rangle$ *him*
		$\langle$−accusative$\rangle$ *he*
	$\langle$+III$\rangle$ $\langle$+female$\rangle$	$\langle$+accusative$\rangle$ *her*
		$\langle$−accusative$\rangle$ *she*
	$\langle$+III$\rangle$ $\langle$−male$\rangle$ $\langle$−female$\rangle$ *it*	
$\langle$−singular$\rangle$	$\langle$+I$\rangle$	$\langle$+accusative$\rangle$ *us*
		$\langle$−accusative$\rangle$ *we*
	$\langle$+II$\rangle$ *you*	
	$\langle$+III$\rangle$	$\langle$+accusative$\rangle$ *them*
		$\langle$−accusative$\rangle$ *they*

Examples of pronouns with their features marked are

$$
\text{her} \quad
\begin{bmatrix}
\text{+N} \\
\text{+pronoun} \\
\text{+III} \\
\text{+singular} \\
\text{+accusative} \\
\text{+female}
\end{bmatrix}
\qquad
\text{they} \quad
\begin{bmatrix}
\text{+N} \\
\text{+pronoun} \\
\text{+III} \\
\text{−singular} \\
\text{−accusative}
\end{bmatrix}
$$

A recent, though not universally accepted, theory is that VERBS and ADJECTIVES are not wholly different constituents in the DEEP STRUCTURE of sentences. Instead, they are considered as *verbals* ($\langle$+VB$\rangle$) and their differences are marked by the features $\langle$+V$\rangle$ for verbs and $\langle$−V$\rangle$ for adjectives. Thus, "run" and "good" would be marked in these ways:

$$
\begin{bmatrix}
\text{run} \\
\text{+VB} \\
\text{+V}
\end{bmatrix}
\qquad
\begin{bmatrix}
\text{good} \\
\text{+VB} \\
\text{−V}
\end{bmatrix}
$$

Verbs and adjectives seem to share some properties. For instance, as there are action verbs and non-action verbs like "walk" and "own," so there are action and non-action adjectives like "honest" and "short." The difference between action ($\langle$+action$\rangle$) and non-action ($\langle$−action$\rangle$) verbals (verbs and adjectives) can be seen in several ways. First, only action verbals can occur in imperative sentences. Non-action verbals cannot:

walk down the street
be *honest*
*own the dog
*be short

Second, only action verbals may take the progressive aspect. Non-action verbals cannot:

> the man is *walking* down the street
> he is being *honest*
> *the man is *owning* the dog
> *he is being *short*

Third, action verbals can occur in some embedded sentences in which non-action verbals cannot occur. This restriction depends upon the verb. Consider sentences with the verb *ask:*

> He asked the girl to *walk* away.
> He asked Jim to be *honest.*
> *He asked the girl to *own* the cat.
> *He asked Jim to be *short.*

The features for the four verbals above would be:

$$
\begin{bmatrix} \text{walk} \\ +\text{VB} \\ +\text{V} \\ +\text{action} \end{bmatrix}
\begin{bmatrix} \text{own} \\ +\text{VB} \\ +\text{V} \\ -\text{action} \end{bmatrix}
\begin{bmatrix} \text{honest} \\ +\text{VB} \\ -\text{V} \\ +\text{action} \end{bmatrix}
\begin{bmatrix} \text{short} \\ +\text{VB} \\ -\text{V} \\ -\text{action} \end{bmatrix}
$$

Adapted from R. Jacobs and P. S. Rosenbaum, *English Transformational Grammar* (Waltham, Mass.: Blaisdell Publishing Co., 1968), pp. 63–64. (See *syntactic markers* under DICTIONARY.)

REFERENCES: N. Chomsky, *Aspects of the Theory of Syntax* (Cambridge, Mass.: MIT Press, 1965); C. J. Fillmore and I. Lehiste, *Working Papers in Linguistics,* No. 2 (Columbus: The Ohio State University, 1968); J. J. Katz, *The Philosophy of Language* (New York: Harper & Row, 1966); J. J. Katz and J. A. Fodor, "The Structure of Semantic Theory," in J. A. Fodor and J. J. Katz (eds.), *The Structure of Language, Readings in the Philosophy of Language* (Englewood Cliffs: Prentice-Hall, 1964).

lexicon   A list or book containing the words of a given language; it is a DICTIONARY. *TG:* The lexicon is the second part of a phrase-structure grammar. It is the source of words that are substituted for the abstract symbols in the TERMINAL STRING. For an example of the application of the lexicon, see DERIVATION. Substitution of words from the lexicon is one of several ways of interpreting a terminal string. (See DICTIONARY, TERMINAL STRING.)

lexicography   A branch of the discipline of linguistics having to do with the making of dictionaries.

linguist   A person whose task it is to analyze and classify the facts of language; a specialist in linguistics. Popularly, a linguist is a person who has command of several languages.

linguistics   A term that denotes the systematic and, frequently, scientific study of language. This discipline has numerous branches such as psycholinguistics, historical (diachronic) linguistics, descriptive (synchronic) linguistics, comparative linguistics, dialectology, and lexicography.

linguistic atlas   A set of maps and tables that report the dialect of a particular geographic region. Examples are *The Linguistic Atlas of New England* and *The Linguistic Atlas of the Upper Midwest.* (See ISOGLOSS, MIDLAND DIALECT.)

REFERENCE: H. Kurath *et al., Linguistic Atlas of New England* (Providence: Brown University, 1939–43).

linking verb   *CG:* A verb that functions mainly in connecting its subject with a predicate adjective or predicate noun. The most common linking verb is *be* when it is used as a full verb:

He *is* fine.
He *is* president.

Other high-frequency linking verbs are *become, remain, seem, look, sound. Str:* Linking verbs are those for which *be* can be substituted without change in the structure meaning of the sentence:

milk *becomes* sour : milk *is* sour
but not
he *found* my dog : he *is* my dog

TG: Linking verbs, like *be,* can be followed by a range of predicate words; these must generally agree in number with the subject noun. Linking verbs, unlike *be,* cannot be inverted to form yes/no questions; thus they are a separate class of verbs from *be*:

He *is* fine : *Is* he fine?
but not
He *remains* tired : **Remains* he tired?

Further subdivision of this conventional class is possible. *Stay* and *remain* differ from *become,* which cannot be immediately followed by adverbs of location:

*He becomes there.

Thus, in transformational grammar, only those verbs that have adjectives immediately after them are linking verbs:

The man *felt* tired.
His face *turned* blue.
The boys *appeared* strong.

Two transformational rules that express these restrictions follow. The first rule separates *be* from all other classes of verbs:

$$MV \rightarrow \begin{Bmatrix} BE + Predicate \\ V_b \end{Bmatrix}$$

The second rule expands V_b (all other verbs) by stating how *stay* and *remain, become,* linking verbs, and all other verbs (V) that are left over from this division are distinct from one another:

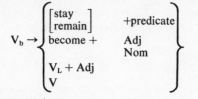

(See COPULATIVE VERB.)

loan word   Words that come into a language through the process of borrowing, a process by which one language absorbs words and expressions from other languages and adapts them to its own particular use. English is one of the world's "borrowingest" languages. Loan words from Latin (exemplified by *animal*), from Greek (*church*), from French (*cattle*), and from the Scandinavian languages (*husband*) are most frequent in English. Minor borrowings into English are exemplified by *clan* from Gaelic, *spook* from Dutch, *paprika* from Hungarian, *vodka* from Russian, *yogurt* from Turkish, *manna* from Hebrew, *chess* from Persian, *algebra* from Arabic, *shampoo* from Hindi, *zebra* from Congolese, *sugar* from Sanskrit, *tea* from Chinese, *kapok* from Javanese, *ketchup* from Malay, *ukulele* from Hawaiian, and so on.

REFERENCES: O. Jespersen, *Growth and Structure of the English Language* (Garden City: Doubleday, 1955; Anchor A46); M. S. Serjeantson, *A History of Foreign Words in English* (London: Routledge and Kegan Paul, 1961; New York: Barnes and Noble, 1961).

localism   A word restricted to a given geographical area. Thus, *cabinet* is a localism in the Narragansett Bay area of southern New England meaning what elsewhere would be called a milkshake, a frosted, a frappe, etc. *Gum band* in the Pittsburgh area describes what is in many other parts of the country a rubber band.

locative   *TG:* An adverbial of place, of location: *in the house, there, at the party.* The pro-form indicating location is SOMEPLACE. In some models of tranformational grammar locative adverbs are introduced in the BASE RULE that expands the main-verb:

$$MV \rightarrow V \ (Adv)$$

(See PRO-FORM.)

low vowel   A vowel produced with the tongue low in the mouth, which is relatively wide open. (See OPEN VOWEL, VOWEL.)

M

main clause sentence *TG:* A basic sentence that can be expanded by receiving an insert sentence through the process of embedment transformation.

> *Main Clause Sentence:* Joe is a man (COMP) ⎱
> *Insert Sentence:* Joe is old ⟹ who is old ⎰ ⟹
> *Result Sentence:* Joe is a man who is old.

(See CONSUMER SENTENCE, MATRIX SENTENCE.)

marker A marker can be considered as a morpheme or a morpheme-combination that indicates the class or grammatical function of a word that includes it. Thus, *-est* indicates the form-class adjective when attached to an adjective base like *grand; -ing* indicates, marks, the form-class verb when attached to a verb base like *eat.* Conjunctions such as *and, or* mark a relationship between two form-classes; thus they are markers. *The* and *a* are markers in that they identify a following noun. Auxiliary verbs such as *must, can* mark following main verbs. Qualifiers like *very, too* mark following adjectives and adverbs. (See PHRASE MARKER, DETERMINER, QUALIFIER.)

mass noun *CG:* The names of materials in general: *gold, coffee, water,* etc. *TG:* A subclass of concrete nouns that are not counted as separate units or as singular or plural. Thus, they do not take the *-s* plural suffix. Some mass nouns are abstract; they name a quality or concept rather than an object: *love, intelligence, honor,* etc. Mass nouns go with *how much* : *how much water, how much intelligence.* Many of them cannot be preceded by the indefinite article in the singular: **a blood, *a gold.* (See COUNT NOUN.)

matrix sentence The same as MAIN CLAUSE SENTENCE, CONSUMER SENTENCE.

metalinguistics In one sense, a branch of linguistics that deals with the relationship between language and such other kinds of culturally determined behavior as gestures. In another sense, metalinguistics refers to the technical language used in making logical and scientific statements about such things as mathematics, philosophy, and language itself.

metathesis The transposition of speech sounds, of a consonant and a vowel. In English the most common metathesis occurs between /r/ and a following vowel: *pretty* /pərti/; *hundred:* /həndərd/; *apron:* /epərn/; *pronounce:* /pərnauns/. Examples of other frequent metatheses in English are *tragedy:* /trædəji/; *relevant:* /rɛvələnt/; *ask:* /æks/. In word history metathesis has been responsible for changing some spellings and pronunciations over the centuries:

Middle English (1100–1400)	Modern English
brid	bird
thridda	third
gærs — græs	grass
clapsen	clasp
drit	dirt

Middle English   The term describes a period in the development of the English language and the language within that period, c. 1100 to 1400.

REFERENCES: J. W. Clark, *Early English: A Study of Old and Middle English* (New York: Norton, 1957); A. MacLeish, *The Middle English Subject-Verb Cluster* ('s-Gravenhage: Mouton, 1969); S. Moore, *Historical Outlines of English Sounds and Inflections*, rev. by A. H. Marckwardt (Ann Arbor: Wahr, 1957); F. Mossé, *A Handbook of Middle English*, J. A. Walker, trans. (Baltimore: The Johns Hopkins Press, 1952); T. F. Mustanoja, *A Middle English Syntax, Part 1: Parts of Speech* (Helsinki: Société Néophilologique, 1960); J. Wright and E. M. Wright, *An Elementary Middle English Grammar* (London: Oxford University Press, 1932).

Midland dialect   A dialect of the English language during the Middle English period. Its boundary was the same as that of the Mercian dialect of Old English, roughly between the Thames River on the south and the Humber River on the north, and from the English Channel to

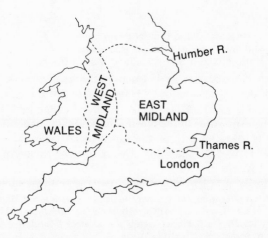

Adapted from Samuel Moore, *Historical Outlines of English Sounds and Inflections*, rev. by Albert H. Marckwardt (Ann Arbor: Wahr, 1960), p. 112.

Wales. It existed in two distinctly different parts, East and West Midland. Because it was the dialect of London, the East Midland Dialect became the predominant dialect of England. It is the ancestor dialect of American English.

In the study of American English dialects, scholars have delineated the Midland area of America as one of three main dialect regions:

A-A: Northern-Midland Dialect Boundary
B-B: Midland-Southern Dialect Boundary
C-C: North Midland-South Midland Dialect Boundary

The dialect boundaries on this map are the result of work done on the dialects of the Atlantic states by Hans Kurath and Raven I. McDavid, Jr., on *The Linguistic Atlas of New England* edited by Hans Kurath, on the Linguistic Atlas of the North-Central States under the direction of Albert H. Marckwardt, on the Linguistic Atlas of the Upper Midwest under Harold B. Allen, and of work done on Southern dialects by Gordon R. Wood.

REFERENCES: H. B. Allen, "The Primary Dialects of the Upper Midwest," in H. B. Allen (ed.), *Readings in Applied English Linguistics,* rev. ed. (New York: Appleton-Century-Crofts, 1964); S. Moore, S. B. Meech, and H. Whitehall, *Middle English Dialect Characteristics and Dialect Boundaries* (Ann Arbor: University of Michigan Press, 1935).

mid verb   *TG:* The mid verbs stand somewhere amidst transitive, intransitive, and linking verbs and the verb *be.* They are a small class of a dozen or so verbs like *cost, have, weigh, lack,* which exhibit the following characteristics:

(1) they must be followed by a noun phrase: *It costs a dollar.*
(2) they cannot be passive like transitive verbs: *A dollar was cost by it.*
(3) they cannot be modified by adverbs of number: *It cost a dollar slowly.*
(4) they differ from *be* and linking verbs in that the number of the noun-object is not controlled by the number of the subject: *He lacked shoes/a shoe.*
(5) they differ from transitive verbs in that they cannot be followed by an *of* construction:

Transitive verb: Joe's building *of the house* delighted her.
Mid verb: *Its costing of a dollar* delighted her.

minimal pair The term describes a pair of words that differ in only one phoneme: /pɪt/ : /bɪt/ ; /pæt/ : /pat/. (See PHONEME.)

modal auxiliary There are ten modal auxiliaries:

can	could
may	might
shall	should
will	would
must	ought to

In sentences they precede verb stems and give them special shades of meaning such as futurity, possibility, volition, probability, permission, necessity, etc. Most frequently, they express a notion of futurity as well as nuances of meaning exclusive of time.

You *ought* to go. *May* I help you?
You *must* run. *Will* you come over?
Could I come over? *Would* you come over?
Can you go away? You *ought to* be careful.

(See AUXILIARY VERB.)

Modern English The term describes the English language from c. 1500 to the present. Early Modern English, the language of Shakespeare, means English from c. 1500 to 1750. Late Modern English refers to English from c. 1750 to the present.

REFERENCES: For Early Modern English see: E. A. Abbott, *A Shakespearian Grammar* (London: Macmillan, 1888; New York; Dover, 1966); T. Pyles, *The Origins and Development of the English Language* (New York: Harcourt, Brace & World, 1964), Chs. 7, 8; M. Schlauch, *The English Language in Modern Times (Since 1400)* (Warsaw: Pánstwowe Wydawnictwo Naukowe, 1959); for Present-day English, see titles under MORPHOLOGY, SENTENCE PATTERN, STRUCTURAL GRAMMAR, SYNTAX, TRADITIONAL GRAMMAR, TRANSFORMATIONAL GRAMMAR, VERB.

modification The function performed by MODIFIERS, which describe or limit the word they are related to.

modifiers Words of several classes (adjectives, adverbs, verbs, determiners, qualifiers) and word groups that function as these words. Modifiers limit and make more precise the meanings of HEADWORDS:

Adjective:	*blue* boat
Adverb:	walk *slowly*
Verb:	*burned* steak, *running* water
Determiner:	*these* men
Qualifier:	*very* good
Word Group:	kitten *in the basket*
	man *whom I saw*

monophthong   A phoneme produced as a single sound. Many vowels and consonants that have a single articulatory position are monophthongs. Compare with DIPHTHONG.

mood   (Sometimes *mode.*) The construction or function of the verb that indicates whether a writer or speaker regards his utterance as a statement (indicative mood), a question (interrogative mood), a command (imperative mood) or an expression of wish, doubt, or possibility (subjunctive mood).

morpheme   A word or part of a word that conveys grammatical or lexical meaning, that cannot be subdivided into smaller meaningful elements, and that occurs in various contexts with a relatively stable meaning. It is often defined as the minimum meaningful unit of language. The morphemes in *unmanly* are *un-, man,* and *-ly.* (See ALLOMORPH, BASE, BOUND MORPHEME, FREE MORPHEME, STEM.)

morphographemic   The term that describes spelling changes that result from a combination of written or printed allomorphs. For example, when *-est* is added to *holy,* the final *y* changes to *i,* resulting in the spelling *holiest;* when *-d* is added to *lay,* the root vowel *a* changes to *ai* and *y* disappears, resulting in the spelling *laid.* These are morphographemic changes. (See GRAPHEME, MORPHOPHONEMIC.)

morphological conditioning   This is largely the result of historical development. For example, the plural morpheme {-s₂} has the morphologically conditioned allomorphs /ɪn/ and /∅/ which are in complementary distribution. The occurrence of these allomorphs is not determined by phonological environment, but rather by the history of the words with which they occur. /ɪn/ occurs today only on *oxen.* The *-en* plural comes from the Old English weak plural ending *-an.* /∅/ allomorph marks the plural on animal words: *swine, sheep, deer, pike,* etc. *Swine,* for example, had only a plural in the genitive case in Old English *swyna.* With the leveling of inflections, this genitive plural disappeared and the word did not take on a nominative and accusative plural /s/ by analogy. (See COMPLEMENTARY DISTRIBUTION, PHONOLOGICAL CONDITIONING.)

morphology   That part of a language concerned with the structure and form of words, with the way in which their morphemes are arranged and related to each other. (See GRAMMAR, MORPHEME.)

REFERENCES: G. O. Curme, *Parts of Speech and Accidence* (Boston: Heath, 1935); H. Marchand, *The Categories and Types of Present-Day English Word-Formation* (Wiesbaden: Harrassowitz, 1960).

morphophonemic   A term that describes a change, or changes, in sound resulting from a combination of allomorphs. For example, when the *-an* of *woman* becomes the plural allomorph *-en, women,* the first vowel changes in pronunciation from /ʊ/ to /ɪ/; when the plural allomorph *-s* is added to *knife,* the consonant /f/ changes to /v/, resulting in the pronunciation /naivz/.

multiple-complex transformation   *TG:* The process in which, when two or more positions are open in a main-clause sentence, two or more insert sentences can be introduced into this main-clause sentence:

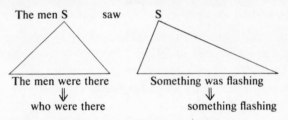

The men S   saw   S

The men were there   Something was flashing
⇓   ⇓
who were there   something flashing

Readout: The men who were there saw something flashing.

(See RECURSIVE COMPLEX TRANSFORMATION.)

mutation   See UMLAUT.

N

nasal consonant   Nasal consonants are articulated like stops, but because the velum is open, the sound is emitted through the nasal cavity. The nasal consonants of English are /m/, the bilabial nasal, /ŋ/, the alveolar nasal, and /n/, the velar nasal. (See CONTINUANT.)

negative transformation   *TG:* A transformation by which a negative sentence is derived from a non-negative sentence by attaching the negative particle *not/n't* to an auxiliary verb. If the source sentence does not have an auxiliary verb (modal, *have*, or *be*), then the verb *do* is introduced to carry tense and the negative particle unless the main verb of the sentence is *be:*

John past see the car ⇒ *John past NEG see the car* ⇒ *John do past NEG see the car* ⇒ *John didn't see the car* (not **John sawn't the car*); but, also, *John present be a car* ⇒ *John present NEG be a car* ⇒ *John isn't a car.*

Any English sentence can be made negative by this simple transformation. The rule looks like this:

$$
NP + tense + \left\{ \begin{array}{l} Modal \\ have \\ be \end{array} \right\} + VP \Rightarrow NP + tense + \left\{ \begin{array}{l} Modal \\ have \\ be \\ do \end{array} \right\} + NEG + VP
$$

neutralization of vowels   Before the end of the Old English period, every unstressed *a, e, o,* and *u* tended to become a vowel, usually spelled *e* and pronounced as /ə/. Thus, all of these unstressed vowels were neutralized. Since the sixteenth century, all English unstressed vowels have been neutralized to either /ə/ or /ɨ/. (See GRADATION.)

node   *TG:* The nodes of a labeled-tree-diagram are the points from which branchings occur.

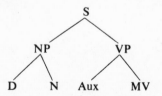

Nodes are said to "dominate" the construction branching from them; thus the S node dominates the NP node and the VP node, etc.

nominal   A noun, pronoun, adjective, adverb, verb participle, or a syntactic construction in a shared position usually filled by nouns. These shared positions are called *subject of the verb, object of the* *verb, object of the preposition, subjective complement, object comple-ment, indirect object.*

Noun:	*John* ran; saw *John;* of *water.*
Pronoun:	*He* is; likes *her,* of *it.*
Adjective:	*Red* is; likes *red;* of *red.*
Adverb:	*Steadily* is the best way to work.
Participles:	*Swimming* is fun; likes *swimming;* of *swimming.*
Construction:	*That he is here* is obvious. I see *that you are here.*

nominative case   A term from the grammar of classical languages designating a word that is the subject of a verb. English has six distinctive pronoun forms that are used as subject: *I, he, she, we, they,* and *who.* Since nouns have no distinctive forms to show that they are subjects of verbs, this function is indicated in English by word order. (See CASE, EXPLETIVE, SUBJECT.)

nonce word   A word coined to suit a particular occasion, often by different writers or speakers, but not generally accepted into the vocabulary. Nonce words are generally here today and gone tomorrow. Many blends are nonce words. (See BLENDING.)

nonhuman nouns   *TG:* A subclass of animate nouns that generally co-occur with the pronouns *that/which.*

dog *that* I saw
animal *which* I saw

(See LEXICAL PROPERTIES.)

nonrestrictive modifier   Nonrestrictive words, phrases, or clauses add descriptive detail about a noun but do not limit or specify its meaning. These modifiers are usually set off by commas and can be omitted from the sentence without changing its basic meaning:

My father, *who was here yesterday,* is fine.
My father, *hale and hearty,* was here yesterday.

A modifier that follows a proper noun is considered to be nonrestrictive, since the name itself limits the person or place:

Bill, *who is standing in the corner,* is fine.
Jamestown, *my home town,* is a pretty place.

(See RESTRICTIVE MODIFIER.)

normative grammar   A prescriptive grammar based on the assumption that there is a universal standard of correctness for all speech and writing.

noun   *CG:* A noun names a person, place, idea, or thing. *Str.* and *TG:* A form-class word that can be inflected for plural with -*s* (cat*s*) and for the possessive with -*'s* (boy*'s*). It can be derived from other words by suffixes such as *-ment* (agree*ment*), *-ity* (abili*ty*), *-ness* (friendli*ness*), and *-ism* (national*ism*.) Nouns exhibit number concord with finite verbs, with determiners, and with some noun modifiers: (*boy works, those men, woman driver/women drivers*). Nouns pattern after determiners (*the/ a man*), after single word modifiers (*tall tree*), before finite verbs in declarative sentences (*The old man lives*), after prepositions (*of water*), and sometimes before other nouns (*telephone operator, dog kennel*). (See LEXICAL PROPERTIES.)

noun adjunct   A noun used in an adjectival position: *telephone* operator, *stone* wall. (See ADJECTIVAL.)

noun clause   A dependent construction, with a subject and predicate, that functions as a noun. Many noun clauses are introduced by a relative connector like *that, which, who, what, why, when,* etc. Noun clauses without these relative words are *reduced noun clauses.*

Subject:	*That he succeeded* pleased him.
Object:	He knows *what he likes.*
Object of Preposition:	She's going to *where she came from.*
Appositive:	The idea *that he should study* is strange to him.
Reduced Clause:	I know the man *you saw yesterday.*

(See DEPENDENT CLAUSE, RELATIVE CLAUSE.)

noun complement position   *TG:* The noun complement position is immediately after a main-clause noun. It may be filled only by an insert sentence having the same noun as the one to be complemented. The noun complement position is an optional one, that is, it does not have to be filled.

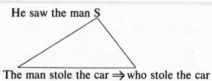

He saw the man S

The man stole the car ⇒ who stole the car

Readout: He saw the man who stole the car.

noun-headed construction   *Str:* This denotes a construction in which a noun is the headword: my old *friend;* my old *friend* whom I saw yesterday. (See HEADWORD.)

noun of quantity   A count noun of quantity names collections, measures, and parts of objects. These nouns occur before *of:*

Collections	*Measures*	*Parts*
a *crowd* of people	a *quart* of milk	a *piece* of cake
a *gang* of thieves	a *pound* of butter	a *slice* of pie
a *group* of boys	a *yard* of silk	a *cut* of meat

noun phrase *CG:* A group of grammatically related words that has the syntactical function of a noun:

> *Subject:* *The old man* walked home.
> *Object:* I saw *the old man.*

TG: A construction in the phrase structure portion of transformational grammar. It consists of an optional determiner, a noun, and the singular or plural number of the noun. This is the rewrite rule for the noun phrase, abbreviated NP:

$$NP \rightarrow (D) + N + N°$$

An NP can be symbolized by a diagram:

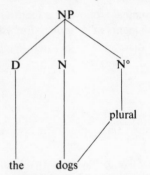

noun replacives Possessive pronouns that can replace NOUN-HEADED constructions indicating possession. Noun replacives are *mine, your, his, hers, ours, theirs.*

> This is my book $\Rightarrow$ This is *mine.*
> This is Jane's book $\Rightarrow$ This is *hers.*

number In English, the difference in word form that shows whether one or more than one person or thing is being referred to. Plural number is usually indicated by -s: tree*s*, river*s*. Singular number is indicated by lack of an ending: tree, river. (See PLURAL INFLECTION.)

O

object   A noun, noun phrase, or other nominal that can be replaced by a personal pronoun in the objective case. Objects follow verbs and prepositions.

> *Direct Object:*   I hit *the man* ⇒ I hit *him.*
> *Indirect Object:*   John gave *the boy* a penny ⇒ John gave *him* a penny.
> *Object of Preposition:*   John gave it to *the boy* ⇒ John gave it to *him.*

(See ACCUSATIVE, CASE.)

objective case   See ACCUSATIVE.

object complement   The second of two nominals following a factitive, or object complement, verb. Object complements in American English can be nouns, adjectives, and infinitive phrases:

> They elected John *president.*
> They painted the house *white.*
> They ordered John *to go.*

(See FACTITIVE VERB, OBJECT.)

obligatory transformation   *TG:* Only the affix transformation is obligatory. (See AFFIX TRANSFORMATION.)

oblique case   A case other than the nominative or vocative. In Classical languages the vocative case indicates the person who is addressed. (See CASE.)

obstruent   A consonant articulated by an obstruction to the flow of air. AFFRICATES, FRICATIVES, and STOPS are obstruents.

Old English   See ANGLO-SAXON.

open syllable   A syllable ending in a vowel sound. (See CLOSED SYLLABLE, SYLLABLE.)

open vowel   The same as a LOW VOWEL. (See LOW VOWEL, VOWEL.)

optative mood   The mood that expresses desire. (See SUBJUNCTIVE MOOD.)

optional element   *TG:* An optional element is enclosed within parentheses; it is an element that does not have to be chosen. For example, the rule

$$S \rightarrow NP + VP \ (Adv)$$

means "Sentence is rewritten as Noun Phrase + Verb Phrase + an optional adverb." This rule, then, accounts for either *He runs* or *He runs slowly.*

optional transformation   *TG:* All transformations except the affix transformation are optional; they are not necessary in generating a grammatical sentence.

oral sound   A sound in which the stream of air is directed into the mouth and which is resonated in the mouth. (See NASAL CONSONANT.)

orthography   The conventional representation of a spoken word in alphabetic writing.

P

palatal sound   Any kind of consonant articulated by placing the tongue front near or against the hard palate: /š ž č j y/ are palatals; /g k ŋ/ are palatalized velar sounds.

palatalization   The adaptation of the point of articulation of a consonant to the place of articulation of a front vowel near it. /k/ can be articulated at the velum when it is followed by a back vowel as in *cool.* It can be palatalized, articulated forward near the palate, when it is followed by a front vowel as in *keel.* Contrast velar /g/ in *goose* with palatal /g/ in *geese.* During the historical development of English, palatalization took place in the south of England more frequently than in the north. Thus, we still find unpalatalized northern forms contrasting with palatalized southern standard forms. Some examples follow.

Northern English	Standard English	Palatalization
kirk	church	/k/ → /č/
garth	yard	/g/ → /y/
scoot (U.S.)	shoot	/sk/ → /š/

paradigm   A set of related words having a common base and all the affixes that may be attached to it. Paradigms are of two kinds. The words in the paradigm may differ according to the derivational affixes that are attached. An example of this is a paradigm built on the Latin base *vide: pro + vide, pro + vis + ion, vis + ion, vis + ible, in + vis + ible, in + vis + ibil + ity, vis + abil + ity,* etc. The words in the second kind of paradigm may differ according to the inflectional affixes that are added. This kind of paradigm is usually associated with the "conjugation" of principal parts of regular and irregular verbs:

Infinitive	3rd Sing. Present	Past Tense	Past Participle	Present Participle
sing	sing*s*	s*a*ng	s*u*ng	sing*ing*
laugh	laugh*s*	laugh*ed*	laugh*ed*	laugh*ing*

A paradigm of nouns might look like this:

Singular	Singular Possessive	Plural	Plural Possessive
girl	girl's	girls	girls'
child	child's	child*ren*	children's

Quite obviously, pronouns, adjectives, and adverbs also exhibit both derivational and inflectional paradigms.

parole   An individual's use of language. This concept contrasts with LANGUE. (See IDIOLECT, PERFORMANCE.)

REFERENCE: F. Saussure, *A Course in General Linguistics,* Wade Baskin, trans. (New York: McGraw-Hill, 1966).

parsing   To parse a sentence is to divide it into its component parts, or constituents, and to describe the grammatical functions of and relationships among these parts. The process of parsing is illustrated graphically by diagrams. (See DIAGRAM.)

participle   The present participle ends in *-ing*. The past participle of "regular," or "weak," verbs ends in *-ed*; "irregular," or "strong," verbs make their past participle by changing the root vowel and sometimes by adding *-en: sang-sung; chose-chosen*. Participles may function as part of a verb phrase:

he is runn*ing*

as adjectives:

the runn*ing* boy

as adverbs:

rav*ing* mad

and as sentence modifiers:

Driv*ing* fast, he went over the hill.

In conventional grammar the term denotes *verb* + *ing* or *verb* + *ed* when they are used as adjectives: burn*ing* house/burn*ed* steak. (See GERUND, PRINCIPAL PARTS.)

participial phrase   A word group lacking a finite verb and introduced by a participle: He walked in, *reading a newspaper.*

part of speech   Grammatical functions in sentences are performed by certain classes of words. Generally, each function is performed by a distinctive part of speech. Parts of speech are nouns, verbs, adjectives, adverbs, pronouns, prepositions, conjunctions, determiners, qualifiers, expletives, etc. In *CG* a word's part of speech depends upon its use in the sentence; in *Str* a word's part of speech depends on its form and position.

particle   Uninflected parts of speech. In English they are prepositions, conjunctions, interjection words, and some adverbs like *no, not.*

passive transformation   The passive transformation switches the position of the subject and object noun phrases of a transitive verb, introduces the verb *be* as an auxiliary, changes the main verb to the past participle, and adds *by* optionally in the adverbial position.

The men repair the house ⟹   The house is repaired (by the men).

NP₁ + Aux + Vₜ + NP₂ ⟹ NP₂ + Aux + be + en + Vₜ + (by + NP₁)

(See PASSIVE VOICE.)

passive voice   *CG:* In the passive voice the subject is acted upon. *Str:* The passive voice verb phrase consists of some form of the verb *be* followed by the past-participle form of the verb:

He *is elected.*
The house *was repaired.*

(See ACTIVE VOICE, PASSIVE TRANSFORMATION.)

past participle   Past participles of verbs have several forms. The most frequent forms end in *-ed, -t, -d,* and *-en*: dream*ed*, caugh*t*, bi*d*, begu*n*, aris*en*. The past participle is used with *have, had, has,* and *having* to form verb phrases.

have dream*ed*
had bi*d*
has caugh*t*
having begu*n*

The past participle is also used as an adjective: burn*ed* steak, was burn*ed*. (See PARTICIPLE, PRINCIPAL PARTS.)

past perfect tense   The tense that indicates a time before the simple past. This tense is marked by *had* plus the past participle of the main verb:

He *had* depart*ed*
They *had been*
He *had* been ask*ed*

(See PERFECT TENSE.)

past tense   These forms of verbs regularly end in *-ed*: pass*ed*, pleas*ed*, part*ed*. Their forms for irregular or strong verbs are many: *shrunk/ shrank, kept, led, began, rode, knew,* etc. The past tense occurs alone, not in combination with the forms of *have*. It *shrank*. He *kept* it, etc. (See PAST PARTICIPLE, PRINCIPAL PARTS.)

perfect tense   The three perfect tenses in English are made with a form of the verb *have* followed by the past participle of the main verb. (See PRESENT PERFECT, PAST PERFECT, FUTURE PERFECT.)

performance   A performance grammar, like structural grammar or the grammar of a foreign language in a textbook, describes what we actually produce at a given moment rather than our abstract ability to produce an infinite number of different sentences. (See COMPETENCE.)

periphrastic construction   A construction that accomplishes its purpose by means of a phrase using function words. (This function would otherwise be indicated by word order or inflections.)

Inflected Genitive: The man's car.
Periphrastic Genitive: The car *of* the man.
Word-Order Indirect Object: He gave *the man the money.*
Periphrastic Indirect Object: He gave the money *to* the man.

person   In English, the division of pronouns into three classes to indicate whether the subject is speaking (first person: *I* run), is spoken to (second person: *You* run), or is spoken of (third person: *he/she/it/ they* run(s)).

philology   The study of written and printed texts in order to interpret the linguistic data in them. The philologist re-creates the history of a language from its written documents. Among the most prominent philologists of the nineteenth century were F. Bopp (1791–1867), R. Rask (1787–1832), and J. Grimm (1785–1863). The latter two are often thought of as the founders of scientific historical linguistics. Rask wrote the first systematic grammar of Old Norse and Old English (1811, 1830), and Grimm's *Deutsche Grammatik* (*Germanic Grammar*) (1819–37) is called the start of Germanic linguistics. Bopp, in his *Comparative Grammar* (1833), discovered the principles of comparative grammar. Wilhelm von Humboldt (1767–1835), one of the profoundest thinkers on general linguistic matters, contributed to the theory of the typological development of language in his *Origin of Grammatical Forms and Their Influence on the Development of Thought* (1822). Probably the most influential mid-nineteenth-century figure in linguistics was A. Schleicher (1821–68) who postulated the *Stammbaumtheorie,* or geneological tree model of the relations between the parent language and the known Indo-European languages. (See FAMILY TREE THEORY, WAVE THEORY.)

REFERENCES: E. Mätzner, *An English Grammar,* C. J. Crece, trans. (London: J. Murray, 1880–85); H. Pedersen, *The Discovery of Language,* J. W. Spargo, trans. (Bloomington: Indiana University Press, 1962); R. Peters, *A Linguistic History of English* (Boston: Houghton Mifflin, 1968); T. Pyles, *The Origin and Development of the English Language* (New York: Harcourt, Brace & World, 1964); S. Robertson and F. G. Cassidy, *The Development of Modern English* (Englewood Cliffs: Prentice-Hall, 1954); R. Stevick, *English and Its History* (Boston: Allyn and Bacon, 1968); E. H. Sturtevant, *An Introduction to Linguistic Science* (New Haven: Yale University Press, 1947).

phone   Any speech sound considered as the result of the physical event of articulation without any thought given to how this sound fits into the sound structure of the language. (Contrast with PHONEME.)

phoneme   A speech sound that makes a difference in meaning. It is symbolized within slant lines: /p/. Thus, /p/ and /b/ are phonemes: *p*it : *b*it; they make a difference in meaning. A phoneme is a family of one or more sounds; allophones are varieties of a given phoneme. They are phonetically similar and in complementary distribution. Present-day English has a total of thirty-nine segmental phonemes: vowels, consonants, etc. The suprasegmental phonemes of English are varieties of stress, pitch, and pause. (See ALLOPHONE, MINIMAL PAIR, PHONEMIC TRANSCRIPTION, SEGMENTAL PHONEME, SUPRASEGMENTAL PHONEMES.)

REFERENCES: W. N. Francis, *The Structure of American English* (New York: Ronald Press, 1958); K. L. Pike, *Phonemics* (Ann Arbor: University of Michigan Press, 1947).

phonemic transcription   A graphic record of speech that uses one symbol for each phoneme. Phonemic transcription, then, recognizes only the meaning-changing sounds of a language: /fonɪmɪk trænskrɪpšən/. A system of transcription is necessary because there is not a 1:1 ratio between the sound system and the writing system of Modern English. For example, there are fourteen ways to spell the phoneme /i/, the vowel in *see*: ee, ie, ea, e, e-e, ei, ey, ay, eo, ae, oe, eau, i, and i-e. (See PHONEME, TRANSCRIPTION.)

phonetics   See ACOUSTIC PHONETICS, ARTICULATORY PHONETICS.

phonetic assimilation   See ASSIMILATION.

phonetic/phonemic transcription   See TRANSCRIPTION.

phonological conditioning   When the allomorphs of a phoneme are in complementary distribution and this distribution is determined by a phonological environment, these allomorphs are said to be phonologically conditioned. As an example, consider the allomorphs /-s~-ɪz~-z/ of the plural morpheme {-s₂}. /s/ is added to singular nouns ending with the phonemes /p t k θ f: *maps* /mæps/; *pets* /pɛts/; *kicks* /kɪks/; *moths* /mɔθs/; *muffs* /məfs/. /ɪz/ is added to singular nouns ending in /s z š ž č j/: *kisses* /kɪsɪz/; *roses* /rozɪz/; *lashes* /læšɪz/; *garages* /gəražɪz/; *churches* /čərčɪz/; *judges* /jəjɪz/. /z/ is added to singular nouns ending in any other phoneme: *pills* /pɪlz/; *sums* /səmz/; *pains* /penz/; *rugs* /rəgz/; *beds* /bɛdz/; *labs* /læbz/; *pies* /paiz/; *toes* /toz/. The phoneme with which a noun ends determines which of the three allomorphs is added to make that noun a plural. Thus we say that these allomorphs are phonologically conditioned; their selection is the result of phonological conditioning. (See ALLOMORPH, COMPLEMENTARY DISTRIBUTION, MORPHOLOGICAL CONDITIONING, PLURAL INFLECTION, SANDHI FORM.)

phonology   The sound system of a language or the study of this system. The sound system of a language consists of (1) the inventory of sounds—its phonetic system; (2) the distribution of these sounds—the rules of order—its phonotactic system; (3) the distribution of allophones of phonemes—its phonemic system; (4) the rules for altering the phonemic shape of morphemes in combination (knife-knives)—its morphophonemic system. *CG:* Phonology means "pronunciation" or "phonetics." *SG:* Phonology is the foundation of the grammatical system, the first "level" of the discovery procedure that leads to morphology and on to syntax. *TG:* Syntax is the foundation of the grammatical system, while phonology is one of several ways of representing the surface structure of a sentence.

phrase   *CG:* A word group without a subject-predicate sequence. *Str:* A syntactic construction that is not a structure of predication; it is not a clause or a "sentence pattern." *TG:* A basic sentence consists of two phrases, a noun phrase (NP) subject and a verb phrase (VP) predicate. (See CONSTRUCTION, NOUN-HEADED CONSTRUCTION, VERB-HEADED CONSTRUCTION, GENERATIVE GRAMMAR.)

phrase marker   *TG:* A labeled-tree diagram that represents the immediate constituent structure of a string. This phrase marker, or tree, has labeled nodes and labeled or unlabeled lines that tell us where parts of the string come from. (See TERMINAL STRING, TREE DIAGRAM.)

phrase structure grammar   Another name for GENERATIVE GRAMMAR.

phrase structure rules   See BASE RULES, RULE OF GRAMMAR.

pictogram   A complete or simplified picture representing an act or object—prehistoric cave paintings, for example.

pidgin language   A language characterized by a simplified grammar and vocabulary when compared with the language on which it is based. Further, a pidgin language has no native speakers. One of the major co-existent varieties of English in Hawaii offers an example of a pidgin language. People who speak the pidgin variety of English in Hawaii speak another language as their native tongue: Chinese, Ilicano, Korean, Japanese, Spanish. And this variety of English has a grammar somewhat more simplified than the grammar of Standard English: (1) There is no verb *be* in equational sentences ("This man sick" : "This man *is* sick"); (2) there is a lack of articles ("I want ball" : "I want *the/a* ball"); (3) there is no possessive inflection on nouns ("He see Tom brother" : "He sees Tom's brother"); (4) the simple morphological structure is further evidenced by lack of inflectional endings for plural and tense ("He like three beer" : "He like*s* three beer*s*"); (5) there is a reduction in the number and use of prepositions ("I go Tom house" : "I go *to* Tom*'s* house"). Viewed in another way, this pidgin variety can be identified with the English of immigrants whose native language is other than English. Adapted from a discussion in S. Tsuzaki, "Hawaiian English: Pidgin, Creole, or Dialect?", *Pacific Speech* (December, 1966), pp. 25–28. (See CREOLE LANGUAGE.)

REFERENCES: R. A. Hall, Jr., *Hands Off Pidgin English!* (New York: Albert Daub, 1956); _____, *Pidgin and Creole Languages* (Ithaca: Cornell University Press, 1966).

pitch levels   Pitch is the quality of speech sounds determined by frequency of vibration of sound waves reaching the ear. High and low pitch are relative, and linguists define four levels from high to low: 4 is extra-high; 3 is high; 2 is normal (most utterances move up or down in pitch from this level); 1 is low (the usual pitch at the end of a statement).

^{2}I ^{3}see the man^1

(See SUPRASEGMENTAL PHONEMES.)

pluperfect tense   The same as the PAST PERFECT TENSE.)

plural inflection   The plural form of most nouns is made by adding the written letter *s* to the singular form: *nouns* + *s* = *nouns*. Depending upon the sound that precedes *s*, this inflection can be pronounced in three ways: /z/: fan*s*; /ɨz/: dish*es*; /s/: rat*s*. Three nouns in English preserve very old plural forms in -*en* and -*ren*: ox*en*, child*ren*, breth*ren*. A few nouns make their plural by changing the vowel of the singular form: *goose/geese; man/men; tooth/teeth; mouse/mice,* etc. A small class of nouns naming animals has no plural inflection: *sheep, deer, bear, fowl;* etc. Some nouns from Latin, like *genus,* preserve their Latin plurals, *genera,* though most of these plurals are Anglicized by the general public: *stadium/stadiums.* One class of nouns in common use frequently preserves the gender distinction in both singular and plural: *alumnus/alumni* (masc.): *alumna/alumnae* (fem.). (See MORPHOLOGICAL CONDITIONING, PHONOLOGICAL CONDITIONING.)

portmanteau word   A result of BLENDING. (See also NONCE WORD.)

position   *Str:* The position of a word in a syntactic construction is the privilege of occurrence that this word has with respect to its environment. Positions are *shared* or *unshared.* A shared position may be one such as prenominal "the _____ house," This position can be shared by nouns (*stone*), adjectives (*gray*), verbs (*burning/burned*), and by inflected nouns (*man's*). An unshared position like "She spoke _____ quickly" can be filled only by qualifiers like *very, too, extremely.* The position is not shared by other word classes.

position class   *Str:* This describes the syntactic class of forms and word groups that occupy shared or unshared positions in sentences. Words and word-groups that fill a position most frequently occupied by nouns are called *nominals*. This position

The _____ is good

can be occupied by nouns (*man*), adjectives (*red*), an indefinite pronoun (*other*), a verb with *-ing* (*meeting*), and by a word group such as *fast runner*. Any word or word group filling the position in the test sentence is a nominal. Words and word groups filling

The _____ ladies are pretty

are *adjectivals*. *Verbals* fill the position

The boy has been _____ happily

Adverbials can fill many positions. One of them is

He reads books _____.

(See POSITION.)

REFERENCE: J. H. Sledd, *A Short Introduction to English Grammar* (Chicago: Scott Foresman, 1959).

positive degree   See COMPARISON.

possessive inflection   The possessive form of most nouns is made by adding the written *'s* for the singular and *s'* for the plural. Depending upon the sound that precedes *'s* or *s'*, they can be pronounced in three ways: /z/: *dog's/dogs'*; /ɨz/: *judge's/judges'*; /s/: *book's/books'*. There are no irregular formations as there are in the plural. The use of the apostrophe in this inflection came about in Shakespeare's time. A word like *boy's* was spelled *boys* or *boyes*. Some writers got the mistaken notion that *the boyes ball* was a contracted form of a construction common in the early seventeenth century, *the boy his ball*. Thus, they used an apostrophe to show that *hi-* had been left out.

postdeterminer   Postdeterminers follow determiners and precede adjectives. This class of words consists of ordinal numbers (the *second* large house), cardinal numbers (the *four* green boats), the possessive of common nouns (the *winter's* last snow) and the following: *every, few, less, little* (quantity), *many (a), more, most, other, same, several, single, such (a)*:

his *every* last wish	those *same* old men
the *many* fine books	any *such* bad jokes
some *other* good guys	Joe's *few* old friends
much *more* coal smoke	the *little* chocolate cake remaining

Not all postdeterminers follow all determiners, but each one may follow at least one determiner. (See DETERMINER, PREDETERMINER.)

postnominal modification   This refers to structures of modification that follow nouns:

> structure of *modification*
> payment *larger than I thought*
> money *to burn*
> meat *cooking slowly*

(See NOUN-COMPLEMENT POSITION.)

predeterminer   A small group of modifiers that pattern before determiners. Predeterminers are words like

> *all* the young boys
> *both* the old men
> *half* the cake
> *double* the money

Phrases like *a few of, none of, one of, some of, pieces of, yards of,* etc., frequently predetermine noun phrases: *a few of those fish, none of the girls, one of the cars,* etc. The word *of* used in this position is called a predeterminer *of;* it is always the last word in a predeterminer. (See DETERMINER, POSTDETERMINER.)

predicate   A structure consisting of at least one or more finite verbs. Objects, complements, and modifiers of the verb are also part of the predicate: *run, run and swim; run and swim all day; gave John a ride in my car yesterday; is well today,* etc.

predicate noun   Also known as predicate nominative, this is a noun that appears after *be* and some linking verbs. This is called the predicate position: He is *president;* He remains *manager;* He seems a *friend.*

predicate adjective   A predicate adjective is an adjective that appears after *be* and many linking verbs: He is *sick;* It smells *sour;* It tastes *bad;* It sounds *good;* etc.

predicate objective   The same as OBJECT COMPLEMENT.

predication   The function of a full verb in a sentence or clause. One of the SYNTACTIC structures. (See PREDICATE.)

prefix   Prefixes are bound morphemes that are attached before bases. There are about seventy-five prefixes in English, and their meanings are frequently like those of prepositions and adverbs: *anti*climax, *co*-pilot, *contra*dict, *de*value, *in*secure, *un*wary, *sub*way, etc.

preposition   Prepositions are a class of function words in English. They are usually followed by a noun, personal pronoun, or a construction, all of which are called the object of the preposition. The most frequently used prepositions are *at, by, for, from, in, of, on, to,* and *with.* Of these, the most frequent are *of, in, to.* Two-syllable prepositions are words like *after, behind, except, inside, under,* etc. Compound, or phrasal, prepositions are constructions like *together with, out of, away from, because of, in spite of, by way of, in reference to, by means of,* etc.

preposition adverb   These are words conventionally classified as prepositions which can also function as adverbs of place: *in, on, out, up, down, over, under, inside, around.*

prepositional phrase   A construction consisting of the preposition and its object. Prepositional phrases can function as adverbials of motion:

ran *into the house*

as adverbs of manner:

ran *with his shoes off*

as adverbs of place:

stood *on the grass*

as noun modifiers:

girl *with a smile;* man *on the street;* bucket *of water*

as predicate nouns:

He was *of the same opinion.*

as noun-subjects:

Under the table was where we found Norman.

prescriptive grammar   The grammar found in many school grammar books. This grammar requires strict adherence to a set of rules that is supposed to be necessary for correctness. Many prescriptive grammars do not discriminate between grammar, in the narrower sense, and usage; thus they also contain prescriptive attitudes toward usage. (See NORMATIVE GRAMMAR.)

present participle   Present participles of verbs end in *-ing.* The present participle is used with *am, is, are, was, were, be, been* to form verb phrases: *were going, been walking,* etc. Present participles are also used as adjectives: *crying* baby, was *sleeping.* (See PRINCIPAL PARTS.)

present perfect tense   The tense that indicates a time before the present but after the simple past. This tense is marked by *has* or *have* plus the past participle of the main verb:

He *has* depart*ed.*
They *have* depart*ed.*
He *has* been ask*ed.*

(See PARTICIPLE, PERFECT TENSE.)

present tense   The present tense of the verb is indicated by the stem form (*depart*) for all persons except the third person singular, which is inflected with *s* (depart*s*). This *s* inflection has the same three phonologically conditioned allomorphs as the plural and possessive morphemes on nouns: /s/: *departs;* /z/: *burns;* /ɨz/: rush*es.*

prestige dialect   The dialect within a speech community which is considered to be "standard" and which is used by cultured speakers within that community. The evaluation "prestige" is cultural and social; it does not mean that one dialect is more systematic than any other. (See DIALECT, USAGE.)

preterit tense   The tense that indicates action in the past without any implication as to its duration. For example: We *swam* there last summer.

preterit-present verbs   These Germanic verbs are irregular. They are called preterit-present because the present tense of each was formerly a strong preterit that lost its preterit meaning and acquired a present meaning. To compensate for this loss of preterit meaning, the new present form acquired an accompanying new weak preterit and past-participle form. Preterit-present verbs retained in Modern American English are *can, shall, may, ought,* and *must.* The last two have no separate preterit form; the other three have *could, should* and *might* as preterit forms. (But see MODAL AUXILIARY.)

primary stress   See STRESS, SUPRASEGMENTAL PHONEMES.

principal parts   The principal parts of verbs can be illustrated in the verb paradigm. Verbs have three, four, or five forms for their principal parts. Verbs with four forms are most frequent.

Stem	Pres. 3rd Sing.	Pres. Ppl.	Past Tense	Past Ppl.
set	sets	setting	set	set
walk	walks	walking	walked	walked
see	sees	seeing	saw	seen

For the use of the principal parts see PRESENT TENSE, PRESENT PARTICIPLE, PAST TENSE, PAST PARTICIPLE.

pro-form   *TG:* In an early model of the grammar, a device used in complex transformations to indicate the place in a main-clause sentence that can be filled by a transformed insert sentence. PRO-forms thus suggest a relationship between a main-clause sentence and one or more insert sentences. They are fillers that indicate the general content of insert sentences when we lack the specific information that these insert sentences contain.

There are three kinds of PRO-forms: those that fill nominal positions, those that fill the noun-complement position, and those that fill adverbial positions. Nominal positions that can be filled by transformed insert sentences are subject, direct object, indirect object, subject complement, object complement, and object of the preposition. The PRO-forms that fill these positions are SOMETHING and SOMEONE.

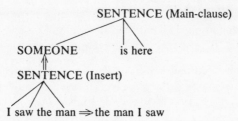

SENTENCE (Main-clause)

SOMEONE   is here
↑↑
SENTENCE (Insert)

I saw the man ⟹ the man I saw

Readout: The man I saw is here.

The noun-complement position immediately follows the noun and permits modification of it. The PRO-form that indicates the possibility of noun phrase expansion is N-COMP.

SENTENCE (Main-clause)

We beat the team + N-COMP
↑↑
SENTENCE (Insert)

the team challenged us ⟹
that challenged us

Readout: We beat the team that challenged us.

PRO-forms that indicate adverbial concepts are SOMEPLACE, SOMETIME, IN-SOME-MANNER, IN-SOME-DIRECTION, FOR-SOME-DISTANCE, FOR-SOME-DURATION, WITH-SOME-FREQUENCY, UNDER-SOME-CONDITIONS, etc.

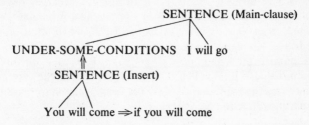

SENTENCE (Main-clause)

UNDER-SOME-CONDITIONS   I will go
↑↑
SENTENCE (Insert)

You will come ⟹ if you will come

Readout: If you will come, I will go.

From another point of view a PRO-FORM is the pronoun which remains after the reduction of an identical element in an embedded sentence or in conjoined sentences. For example, when two identical noun phrases occur in the same sentence a Pronominalization reduces the second one to a pronoun, a PRO-FORM.

Tom saw the car and Joe drove the car ⟹ Tom saw the car and Joe drove *it.*

An embedded clause may be reduced to *this, that,* or *which.* Consider the sentence

> Joe drove the car and that Joe drove the car displeased Tom.

The embedded clause *that Joe drove the car* is, except for *that,* identical to the first clause in the sentence. Because of this identity, the embedded clause can be reduced to a PRO-FORM *this:*

> Joe drove the car and *this* displeased Tom.

(See NOUN-COMPLEMENT POSITION, COMPLEX TRANSFORMATION, IN-SERT SENTENCE, DEPENDENT CLAUSE, MULTIPLE-COMPLEX TRANSFOR-MATION.)

progressive tense　　The tense that represents continuing action, in contrast with a habitual or completed action. The progressive tenses are signaled by some form of *be* and the present participle of the main verb:

> I am going
> She was going
> We have been going
> They will be going

Some linguists use the term *aspect* instead of *tense* in describing the progressive construction. From this point of view, the idea expressed is not so much one of the time of action as it is the notion that the action is incomplete (*durative aspect*) or completed (*punctual aspect*). (See ASPECT.)

pronoun　　Some pronouns are used in place of nouns. Pronouns are of many subclasses: *personal pronouns* with their subject, object, and possessive forms (*I, me, my; we, us our,* etc.), *relative pronouns* (*that, which,* etc.), *noun-replacive* forms of personal pronouns (*mine, yours, theirs,* etc.), *interrogative pronouns* (*who, when,* etc.), *intensive* and *reflexive pronouns* (*myself, himself,* etc.), *demonstrative pronouns* (*this, those,* etc.), and *indefinite pronouns* (*someone, anyone,* etc.). For the most part, pronouns are a form class; that is, they are inflected. In sentences the subject and object personal pronoun forms and the noun-replacives function as nouns:

> Tom saw John ⟹ *He* saw *him.*
> Joan is your girl ⟹ *She* is *yours.*

The possessive forms of personal pronouns pattern like the noun deter-miners *the* and *a: my* book, *his* desk, *your* pen. *Who* is also a relative pronoun along with *what, that, which:*

> *Who* he is I don't know.
> man *who* is outside.

Intensives (He *himself* said so!) and reflexives (He hit *himself* with a hammer) refer to a noun or pronoun already mentioned at least once. (See LEXICAL PROPERTIES.)

proper noun   The name of a particular person, place, or thing: *Joe, Minneapolis, Mardi Gras.* Proper nouns cannot be preceded by either the definite or the indefinite article. (See COMMON NOUN.)

proto-   This word, used in combination, designates the earliest known form of a word of language or the artificially reconstructed original of a word of language. *[swepnos] is a reconstructed word in Proto-Indo-European. (See PROTO-INDO-EUROPEAN.)

Proto-Indo-European   A hypothetical, reconstructed language regarded as the common ancestor of all languages in the Indo-European family. It has been reconstructed from related languages that are apparently its ancestors. (See INDO-EUROPEAN.)

psycholinguistics   The examination of the relationship between the descriptive and the behavioral approaches to the study of language. Psycholinguistics attempts to relate the work of the descriptive linguist, who formulates the rules for generating sentences, with the work of the psychologist, who attempts to determine what factors cause a person to say something in a certain way at a certain time.

punctuation   A system of eleven marks that are written substitutes for the suprasegmental features of speech. (See GRAPHEME, SUPRASEGMENTAL PHONEME.)

Q

qualifier   Sometimes called *intensifiers,* these are words that pattern like *very.* They modify adjectives: *very* good, *too* happy, *pretty* bad. Adverbs are frequently modified by qualifiers: *rather* quickly, *very* slowly. In conventional grammar these words are called adverbs, though they clearly do not pattern as adverbs in position after the verb: "He ran *quickly*" but not "He ran *very.*"

question   An interrogative sentence that can be answered either by *yes* or *no* or by furnishing information relating to *What? Why? When? Where? Who? How?* etc. Yes/No questions can occur grammatically in statement form with a rising intonation: ²You're going³ hóme³↑ or they can occur with subject and verb inverted, usually with rising intonation: ²Are you going³ hóme³↑. If the verb is not a modal auxiliary, *have* or *be,* then *do* asks the question: ²Did he go³ hóme³↑. Information questions are signaled by any one of the "*Wh*-words" listed above: ²Who is³ going¹↓ ; ²Where³ are you¹↓ . *TG:* Both the Yes/No question and the *WH*-question derive from basic sentences by way of a simple transformation: You're going home ⇒ Are you going home?; John is going ⇒ Who is going?; You are there ⇒ Are you there? ⇒ Where are you? (See QUESTION TRANSFORMATION, YES/NO QUESTION, WH-QUESTION.)

question transformation   *TG:* For Yes/No Questions the transformational rule is as follows:

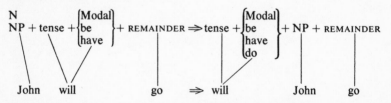

The information question takes many forms since we can question the subject, the object, or other predicate elements. The easiest way to describe this question transformation is to say that it has two parts.

(1) The basic sentence is transformed into a Yes/No Question.
(2) The appropriate *Wh*-word is substituted for the item to be questioned and then put into the initial position in the sentence.

Here are some examples:

(1) Questioning the Subject:
 Basic Sentence: *John* will go.
  Yes/No Q: Will *John* go?
  Wh-word Q: *Who* will go?
(2) Questioning the Object:
 Basic Sentence: John reads *the book.*
  Yes/No Q: Does John read *the book?*
  Wh-word Q: *What* does John read?

(See MODAL AUXILIARY, QUESTION, WH-QUESTION.)

R

received standard pronunciation   The pronunciation of English that is "accepted" among educated people in Britain.

reconstruction   In linguistics the process of determining the original, unwritten form or state of a parent language by comparing written and spoken forms of languages descended from the original. PROTO-INDO-EUROPEAN is a reconstructed language. (See RESIDUE FORMS.)

REFERENCE: H. Hoenigswald, *Language Change and Linguistic Reconstruction* (Chicago: University of Chicago Press, 1960).

recursiveness   A basic quality of the system of any language; it enables the grammar of a language to produce an infinite number of sentences. A language is made up of a relatively small number of basic sentence types that are used recursively, over and over again, to produce complex sentences. A recursive rule, then, is one that enables us to trace our way through a grammar an infinite number of times. In the next definition there is an example of recursiveness. Note that the term *sentence* is itself recursive and that all the rules below the level of *sentence* recur. (See RECURSIVE COMPLEX TRANSFORMATION.)

recursive-complex transformation   The quality of recursiveness, discussed in the definition above, can be illustrated by showing how a complex sentence is formed. Consider this sentence:

John cleaned the shop after he was done so that he could start another job.

It is made up of three simple, basic sentences:

(1) John cleaned the shop SOMETIME FOR-SOME-PURPOSE.
(2) He was done.
(3) He could start another job.

Sentences (2) and (3) are transformed so that they can become sub-sentences, parts, of sentence (1). We can diagram the recursive complex sentence like this (notice, first, that the term SENTENCE is recursive; it is used, it recurs, three times):

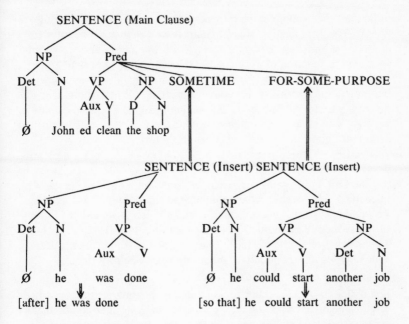

Readout: John cleaned the shop after he was done so that he could start another job.

Notice also the recursiveness in the rules by which the constituents of the three sentences are constructed. The rule NP → D + N recurs four times. The rule VP → Aux + V recurs three times. At an even lower level of construction the rewrite rule for determiner occurs five times:

$$D \rightarrow \begin{Bmatrix} \varnothing \\ the \\ another \end{Bmatrix}$$

And so on. (See RECURSIVENESS, REWRITE RULES.)

redundancy   This term means "something that is said more than once." Languages have redundancy in their grammars and between their grammars and intonation contours. An example of grammatical redundancy can be seen in the sentence *The dog barked at the top of his voice.* The verb *barked* is redundant because its meaning—"make a vocal noise like a dog"—includes the meanings given in the sentence by *dog* and *voice.* A more obvious example can be seen in the duplication of plural signals in the expression *those dogs.* This phrase is marked twice as plural—by the plural pronoun *those* and by the noun-plural ending *-s* on *dog.* Intonation contours and grammar can also be redundant. For example, the intonation features and word order of one type of Yes/No question are redundant—we can predict the intonation contour by knowing the word order. Both intonation and word order perform the function of asking a Yes/No question: ^{2}Are you^3 going^3 ↑. Thus, linguistic redundancy is the excess of linguistic signals above the minimum necessary to convey meaning. When redundancy is present, we can often predict one meaning signal by the presence of another. The built-in redundancies of language are to be distinguished from more controllable redundancies in rhetoric.

reduplication   The process by which languages construct a derivative form or an inflected form by doubling a specified syllable. Illustrations may be found in Tagalog: [ta: wa], "a laugh," reduplicated [ta: ta: wa], "one who will laugh"; Thai reduplicated *dang-dang*, "red, reddish"; Latin *cado*, "I fall," reduplicated *cecidi*, "I fell." Sometimes reduplication is merely euphonic; it has no meaning. For example, in Swedish the usual rejoinder to [tăk], "thanks," is the reduplicated [tăk:tăk], which serves as a euphonious substitute for "You're welcome."

reference of pronouns   See ANTECEDENT.

regional dialect   The major regional dialect boundaries that have been established to date in the United States indicate nine major dialect areas: *Eastern New England* (eastern Massachusetts, eastern Connecticut, Rhode Island, Vermont, Maine); *New York City; Eastern Virginia; Eastern Southern* (eastern North and South Carolina, southern Georgia, southeast Alabama, Florida); *Central Southern* (southeastern Alabama, Mississippi, southern Arkansas, Louisiana, East Texas, southern Oklahoma); *Western Southern* (West Texas); *South Midland; North Midland; Northern.* (See DIALECT, MIDLAND DIALECT.)

relative adverb   These are words like *as, after, before, when, where*. They occur after nouns, introducing a relative clause that functions as an adjective:

the place *where* I saw him
the time *when* he won the game
the house *after* the one you live in

(See RELATIVE CLAUSE.)

relative clause   A clause subordinate to the main clause with which it occurs and to which it is connected by a relative word such as *that, which, what, who, whom*. Relative clauses function as adjectives:

man *whom I saw*

as nouns:

What you don't know won't hurt you.

or as adverbs:

He went *when the sun set.*

(See RELATIVE ADVERB, RESTRICTIVE MODIFIER, NONRESTRICTIVE MODIFIER.)

relative pronouns   These are used to relate and connect relative clauses to one another and to main clauses. They are words like *who, which, that, whom, what,* etc. (See RELATIVE CLAUSE.)

relic area   The area in which geographical or cultural isolation and relative lack of prestige have caused retention of older dialect forms or have prevented the spread of dialect forms characteristic of the area. Relic areas in the United States are northeastern New England, the eastern shore of Chesapeake Bay, and eastern North Carolina. Dialect forms in these areas lack prestige, especially when they are used by older or less sophisticated speakers. (See DIALECT, FOCAL AREA.)

replacive allomorph   Replacive allomorphs contrast with additive allomorphs. Consider the allomorphs of the past-tense morpheme $\{-d_1\}$ which replace the vowels in /sɪŋ tɛr bait gro spik tek/ to produce the past tense forms /sæŋ tɔr bɪt gru spok tʊk/. Thus, we can consider / æ ɔ ɪ u o ʊ/ as some of the replacive allomorphs of $\{-d_1\}$. (See ADDITIVE ALLOMORPH.)

residue forms   These occur during historical reconstruction. After laws of phonetic correspondence among several languages have been postulated, there will remain word forms whose existence cannot be accounted for by these laws. These word forms, then, are residues from the application of the laws of phonetic correspondence. These residual forms that do not fit into recognizable types of phonetic correspondence may be accounted for by the fact that while they may be descendants of a common ancestral form, they may be deviant because we have not correctly determined the phonetic correlation. An instance of this was the supposed deviancy between Sanskrit [bo:dha:mi] and English *bid* before the discovery of GRASSMAN'S LAW concerning the disappearance of aspiration in the first of two successive aspirated stops. Or residue forms may not be descendants of a common ancestral form at all. In this case the resemblance between the residue and a group of apparently related languages may be due to accident: Latin *dies* and English *day* do not represent an etymology that falls within any known set of correlations; nor do Malay [mata], "eye" and Greek [máti]. Resemblance may be due to borrowing of cultural or technical words in general distribution. English-Finnish *abstract-abstraktinen, architect-arkkitehti* exhibit a relationship which is only apparent; there is no kinship between Finno-Ugrian and Indo-European. Sometimes apparent correlations may be due to partial morphological resemblances of word forms in the parent language; Latin *habēre* and English *have* may be descendants of two stems which were morphologically similar in Indo-European. Finally, residue forms may appear resemblant for reasons other than descent from a common prototype. Latin *dentālis* and English *dental*, while they look alike, do not exhibit the Latin *d*: English *t* correspondence indicated of common Indo-European prototypes by the FIRST CONSONANT SHIFT. The reason for the resemblance is that *dental* is an English speaker's pronunciation of the Latin word; there is no prototypical relationship. (See GRASSMAN'S LAW, FIRST CONSONANT SHIFT.)

restrictive modifier   Restrictive words, phrases, or clauses limit or specify the meaning of the nouns they modify, providing information that is essential to the meaning of the sentence. Restrictive modifiers are not set off by commas from the rest of the sentence:

> The man *over here* is the one.
> The car *that I bought yesterday* is newer than my other one.

(See NONRESTRICTIVE MODIFIER.)

retroflex *r*   Speakers of American English pronounce the retroflex r before stressed vowels (*ród, erúpt*), and initially before unstressed vowels (*rèfér, rèmínd*). The tip of the tongue is turned upward toward the hard palate so that it points to, but does not touch, the palatal area immediately behind the alveolar ridge.

rewrite rule   *TG:* The means of representing expansion and/or change. An arrow is used to indicate the operation of rewriting; it is an instruction that the symbol or string of symbols to the left of the arrow is to be rewritten as the string to the right. Thus, the arrow also suggests a relationship between the string on the left and the string on the right. In the phrase structure rules a single-shafted arrow shows the relation "is rewritten as" or "is expanded into." For example, the arrow in the rule NP → D + N indicates that a noun phrase (NP) is rewritten as, or is, a Determiner (D) and a Noun (N). Thus, rewrite rules can expand linguistic units. In the transformational portion of the grammar the double-shafted arrow indicates the relationship "is changed into," "is derived from." For example, the rule $X + Y \Rightarrow Y + X$ indicates that $X + Y$ is changed into $Y + X$, that the relationship between $X + Y$ and $Y + X$ is that $Y + X$ is "derived from" $X + Y$. The passive transformation is an example of a rewrite rule in the transformational grammar:

$$NP_1 + V_t + NP_2 \Rightarrow NP_2 + BE + ed + V_t + (by + NP_1)$$

(See RULE OF GRAMMAR.)

rhotacism   See VERNER'S LAW.

root   See BASE.

rounded vowels   Rounded vowels, like the ones in *boot* and *put,* are produced with a rounding of the lips. In most standard American English dialects the back vowels are round and the front and central vowels are unround. (See VOWEL.)

rule of grammar   Different grammars demand different notions as to what a rule of grammar is. Generally speaking, we can make the following broad distinctions. *CG:* The rule is deductive and prescriptive in its formulation. That is, the rule prescribes linguistic conduct on the basis that there is, somewhere, a standard of correct usage in speech and writing that all levels and varieties of English should adhere to. "Avoid the split infinitive" is an example of this kind of rule. To really write well, one should avoid this construction. Another kind of prescriptive, deductive rule is based on the logical fallacy that the laws of language reflect the logic of the universe outside language. "Never use two negatives, because they make a positive" is an example of this kind of rule. But one can never be sure that he is not using the double negative. A third kind of prescriptive rule is based on rhetoric, not usage or logic: "Avoid the passive voice." Another prescriptive rule is the groundless, sheerly negative prescription "Never end the sentence with a preposition." Sir Winston Churchill once remarked that this was the kind of pedantic interference up with which he would not put. Some rules of this grammar are syllogistic in nature: "Every*one* should put on *his* coat." *Str:* The rules of structural grammar are largely inductive and descriptive. That is, the rule objectively describes a linguistic phenomenon on the basis of wide observation, but it does not attempt to prescribe the "correctness" of a particular usage. Structural rules describe the forms of words and the patterns in which they occur in sentences. An example of a rule describing the forms of words is the following: "English nouns are characterized by what is called the possessive form: *man's, teacher's, Tom's.*" An example of a "pattern" rule is the following: "Some characteristic noun positions are 'The _____ is ugly,' 'I saw their _____,' 'a glass of _____.' Any word occurring in these positions is a nominal." *TG:* The rewrite rules of transformational grammar are deductive in their application; that is, the rules must apply every time the prescribed syntactic conditions occur and the rules must be applied in a fixed sequence. There are two kinds, phrase structure rules and transformation rules. The phrase structure rules expand elements in the phrase structure grammar. They are of the type exemplified by $NP \rightarrow D + N$, which states that a noun phrase is composed of a determiner and a noun. Rules of transformation are of the type exemplified by $X + Y \Rightarrow Y + X$, which states that $X + Y$ is changed to $Y + X$, that the relationship between $X + Y$ and $Y + X$ is that $Y + X$ is derived from $X + Y$. These two types of rules are the syntactic rules of transformational grammar. Their purpose is to describe and account for all and only the grammatical sentences of a language. The rules of conventional and structural grammar parse sentences *after* they have been produced; thus these rules can analyze only a few of the sentences of a language. (See REWRITE RULE.)

runic writing   Runes are characters of the alphabet used by Germanic peoples from approximately the third century A.D. The earliest remaining writings of Old English are written in the runic alphabet. The Old English characters *thorn* (þ) and *wynn* (ƿ) are runic.

S

sandhi form The modification of the sound of a morpheme, of a word, or of an affix. These modifications are conditioned by the phonological context in which the morpheme is uttered. Sandhi variants can be illustrated by the pronunciations of *the* as /ðə/ in *the boy* and as /ði/ in *the old man;* by the pronunciations of plural *s* as /s/ in *cats,* as /z/ in *dogs,* and as /ɪz/ in *dishes;* by the pronunciations of *not* as /nt/ in *can't* and as /nat/ in *cannot.* (See PHONOLOGICAL CONDITIONING.)

satem languages These constitute one of the divisions of the Indo-European family of languages. The satem group is composed of the Indo-Iranian, Armenian, Balto-Slavic, and Albanian languages. In these languages the consonant /s/—as in Avestan *s*atem, Lithuanian *š*imtas, and Old Slavic *s*ŭto, all meaning "hundred"—represents a palatalization of the /k/ found in the centum languages: Latin *c*entum, "hundred." (See CENTUM LANGUAGES, PALATALIZATION.)

school grammar The name given to the prescriptive statements found in most school grammar books. (See PRESCRIPTIVE GRAMMAR.)

schwa The name of a mid-central unstressed vowel. In phonetic transcription it is symbolized by /ə/. Schwa is probably the most frequently occurring vowel in American English. It can be heard in words such as *o*ccur, ang*e*l, *a*side.

segmental phoneme Segmental phonemes are segments of sound, the phonemes arranged in sequence in an utterance, the vowels and consonants. They are contrasted in linguistic description with SUPRA-SEGMENTAL PHONEMES.

semantics In one of its meanings, a branch of linguistics. The term refers to a theory, study, or system of meanings underlying a word, phrase, sentence, or language. These linguistic meanings of the term are different from its meaning in the term GENERAL SEMANTICS. See *TG* definition under DICTIONARY, LEXICAL PROPERTIES.

sememe The semantic meaning of a morpheme. (See MORPHEME.)

semivowel Semivowels are articulated in consonantal positions in the mouth. They are in the same syllable with a full vowel, which is the nucleus of the syllable. Their duration is brief; they consist of a rapid movement of the articulators from a characteristic initial position to the position of the vowel that follows. Or the movement is the reverse, from the position of the preceding vowel to a characteristic final position. Semivowels are sometimes called GLIDES. /w/ is the voiced and voiceless labiovelar semivowel. It is formed by raising the tongue back toward the velum and then moving it rapidly to the position for the next vowel. The degree of lip-rounding depends upon the following vowel. /r/ is the voiced and voiceless apico-alveolar retroflex semi-vowel. The American /r/ is formed in various ways in different dialects. (See RETROFLEX *r*.) /y/ is the voiced fronto-palatal semivowel. It is formed by bringing the tongue front close to the palate where it joins the alveolar ridge, with the tongue tip pointing toward the upper teeth or resting against the lower front teeth. The tongue is then moved rapidly down into the position of the following vowel.

sentence   A sequence of words forming a unit. Actually, there is no simple, clear statement that takes into account the various points of view as to just what a sentence is. More specifically, a sentence is a structure of predication consisting of a noun-phrase subject and a verb-phrase predicate. This structure of predication makes sense to a native speaker and is not contained within another sentence. *CG, Str:* In conventional and structural grammars sentences are classified as simple (consisting of one structure of predication), compound (consisting of two or more coordinate structures of predication), complex (consisting of one independent structure of predication and one or more dependent structures of predication), or compound-complex (two or more coordinate independent structures of predication and at least one dependent structure of predication). Further, structural grammar describes a sentence as a verbal sequence that ends with either a falling terminal juncture, He went home ↓ (statement), or a rising terminal juncture, He went home ↑ (question). A written sentence is, conventionally, an acceptable structure of predication that begins with a capital letter and ends with a period, exclamation mark, or question mark, and is bounded by space. *TG:* In transformational grammar a sentence (S) is rewritten as a noun-phrase plus a verb-phrase: S → NP + VP. A sentence generated by rules in the phrase structure grammar is a simple, active, indicative, affirmative sentence. It is called a basic sentence. All other sentences are derived from basic sentences by simple and complex transformations.

sentence pattern   A basic sentence type is composed of elements in a left-to-right sequence. *Str:* Structural grammar considers a number of sentence patterns based upon the number and kind of elements following the verb and, in part, upon the kind of verb. Six structural sentence patterns may be summarized as follows:

N ↔ V:	Dogs bark.
N ↔ LV Adj:	Elephants seem large.
N ↔ V N:	Monkeys eat bananas.
N ↔ LV N:	Horses are animals.
N ↔ V N N:	John gave Bill a bicycle.
N ↔ OV N N:	John called Bill a fool.

In these patterns, LV is a linking verb, and OV is an object complement verb. An object complement verb is one that makes the two words after it name the same thing. *TG:* Basic sentence patterns in transformational grammar are differentiated by the nature of the verb in the pattern. These are four basic patterns defined in this way:

$NP + be + Pred + (Adv)$:	Bill is happy (today).
$NP + V_i + O + (Adv)$:	Bill sleeps (soundly).
$NP + V_t + NP + (Adv)$:	Bill ate steak (yesterday).
$NP + V_c + Comp + (Adv)$:	Bill seemed sick (last night).

Sentence patterns in *TG* are further determined by the kinds of transformations (changes) these basic sentences can undergo. For example, only the pattern with V_t, the transitive verb, can be changed into a passive sentence. On the basis of subclassifying these four types of verbs and then seeing the kinds of transformations they can undergo, we would probably get ten or twelve basic sentence types. In the representation above, V_i is an intransitive verb, V_t is a transitive verb, and V_c stands for all linking verbs except *be*, which is in the first pattern. The parentheses around (Adv) mean that an adverbial element is optional.

REFERENCES: Paul Roberts, *Patterns of English* (New York: Harcourt, Brace & World, 1956); _____, *English Sentences* (New York: Harcourt, Brace & World, 1962).

sibilant   A fricative consonant. In the production of fricatives, the tongue comes into contact with the hard palate. Sibilants are /s/ (*see*), /z/ (*zest*), /š/ (*ship*), /ž/ (*rouge*), /č/ (*church*), ǰ/ (*joke*).

simple sentence   A simple sentence has one subject-predicate combination that is an independent clause: *Lions roar.* (See COMPOUND SENTENCE, COMPLEX SENTENCE, COMPOUND-COMPLEX SENTENCE.)

simple transformation   A simple transformation operates on one basic sentence or on a terminal string of morphemes, as contrasted with a complex transformation, which operates on two or more basic sentences. All simple transformations are optional except the affix transformations. Some other simple transformations are *passive* (He saw the game ⇒ The game was seen by him), *negative* (He saw the game ⇒ He didn't see the game), *Yes/No Question* (*He is nice* ⇒ Is he nice?), *Wh-Question* (He is here ⇒ Where is he?), *There-Expletive* (The boy is here ⇒ There is a boy here), *Imperative* (You will close the door ⇒ Close the door!). (See AFFIX TRANSFORMATION, NEGATIVE TRANSFORMATION, PASSIVE TRANSFORMATION, THERE-EXPLETIVE TRANSFORMATION, QUESTION TRANSFORMATION.)

singular form   The form that denotes "one." Among nouns that form plurals, the singular form is the one without the plural ending.

slang   Slang is composed of a large body of words and expressions which are intelligible to and frequently used by a large portion of the speakers of a language, though it is not accepted as formal usage. Slang is derived mostly from cant, jargon, and argot words, and its use suggests that both speaker and listener enjoy a kind of mutual understanding. (See ARGOT, CANT, JARGON.)

REFERENCE: H. Wentworth and S. B. Flexner (eds.), *Dictionary of American Slang* (New York: Crowell, 1960).

social dialect   A cultural or technical variant of the language of a speech community. A cultural variant can be exemplified by contrasting the speech of educated speakers with the speech of uneducated speakers. A technical variant can be exemplified by contrasting the technical speech of space scientists, engineers, etc., with the speech of the layman. Social dialects differ from one another in their vocabulary, pronunciation, and grammar. Each speaker of a language probably commands more than one social dialect. (See DIALECT.)

REFERENCES: E. Evertts (ed.), *Dimensions of Dialect* (Champaign: NCTE, 1967); J. L. Fischer, "Social Influences on the Choice of a Linguistic Variant," in H. B. Allen (ed.), *Readings in Applied English Linguistics* (New York: Appleton-Century-Crofts, 1964); W. Labov, "Stages in the Acquisition of Standard English," in R. W. Shuy (ed.), *Social Dialects and Language Learning* (Champaign: NCTE, 1964); _____, *The Study of Nonstandard English* (Champaign: NCTE, 1970); R. I. McDavid, Jr., "American Social Dialects," *College English* 26 (1965):10–16; _____, "Some Social Differences in Pronunciation," in Allen (ed.), *op. cit.;* _____ and Virginia G. McDavid, "The Relationship of the Speech of American Negroes to the Speech of Whites," *American Speech,* 26 (1951):3–17; L. A. Pederson, "Social Dialects and the Disadvantaged," in *Language Programs for the Disadvantaged* (Champaign: NCTE, 1965); W. A. Stewart, *Non-standard Speech and the Teaching of English* (Washington: Center for Applied Linguistics, 1964); _____, "Non-standard Speech Patterns," *Baltimore Bulletin of Education,* 43 (1966–67):2–4, 52–65.

sound change   The term, an historical concept, describes changes in a speech sound or phoneme which are brought about because of characteristics of the sound itself or by influence of nearby sounds. (See ABLAUT, FIRST CONSONANT SHIFT, UMLAUT, VERNER'S LAW.)

source sentence   See CONSTITUENT SENTENCE, INSERT SENTENCE.

spelling pronunciation   An attempt to make pronunciation conform closely to spelling. But spelling is not an infallible guide to pronunciation because of the many irregularities of English orthography. Consider, for example, words like *come/home; move/shove; friend/fiend/ sieve.* Spelling pronunciations frequently came about in the course of the historical development of a word. For example, *alter, fault, vault,* and *Walter* had the thirteenth- and fourteenth-century Middle English spellings *auter, faut(e), vaute,* and *Wat(te).* Thus, they were like the "l-less" Old French words from which they derive. The *l* came into these words through the influence of Latin spelling. They became *vault* in the fifteenth century, and *alter, fault,* and *Walter* in the sixteenth century. In the seventeenth century these words were pronounced irregularly with and without /l/ on the analogy with the varied pronunciations of native words like *malt* and *salt.* Thus, a spelling pronunciation was established, and the pronunciations with /l/ became regular by the eighteenth century.

REFERENCES: J. S. Kenyon, "Spelling Pronunciation," in *American Pronunciation,* 10th ed. (Ann Arbor: Wahr, 1950); A. MacLeish, "Do You Pronounce It As It's Spelled?" in N. C. Stageberg and W. Anderson, *Introductory Readings on Language,* rev. ed. (New York: Holt, Rinehart & Winston, 1970).

spirant   See FRICATIVE.

split infinitive   A grammatical construction in which an adverb occurs between *to* and the verb: *to quietly go, to easily see.* (See RULE OF GRAMMAR.)

Standard English   A term applied to an item of usage or a dialect of English that is acceptable to educated, cultivated speakers of the language. Standard English is the English used to carry on the daily business of the nation.

stem   A linguistic form to which an inflectional suffix can be attached: run/run*s;* beautify/beautif*ied;* agreeableness/agreeableness*es.*

stop   A consonant sound formed by a stoppage and, in many instances, a release of breath. The voiceless stops are /p t kʔ/. The voiced stops are /b d g/. /p/ and /b/ are bilabial stops; they are formed by the lower lip meeting the upper one and stopping the breath. The vocal cords vibrate when /b/ is sounded, thus it is a voiced bilabial stop; /p/ is a voiceless bilabial stop. When /p/ and /b/ occur at the beginning and middle of words, as in *pin, bin, spin, number,* the lips open and release the breath, though with much less force with /b/ than with /p/. When /p/ and /b/ occur at the end of words, as in *stop* and *tub,* the lips stay closed and the breath is unreleased. /t/ and /d/ are alveolar stops. They are formed by the tongue tip coming into contact with the alveolar ridge (the ridge just behind the upper gums) and stopping the breath. The vocal cords vibrate when /d/ is sounded, thus it is a voiced alveolar stop. /t/ is a voiceless alveolar stop. When /t/ and /d/ occur at the beginning and middle of words, as in *top, dog, stop, ladder,* the lips open and release the breath, though with much less force with /d/ than with /t/. When /d/ and /t/ occur at the end of words, as in *sad* and *hot,* the lips stay closed and the breath is unreleased. /k/ and /g/ are velar stops. They are formed by raising the tongue back against the velum, thus stopping the breath. The vocal cords vibrate when /g/ is sounded, thus it is a voiced velar stop. /k/ is a voiceless velar stop. When /k/ and /g/ occur at the beginning and middle of words, as in *kin, go, skin, stagger,* the lips open and release the breath, though with much less force with /g/ than with /k/. When /g/ and /k/ occur at the end of words, as in *beg* and *lick,* the lips stay closed and the breath is unreleased. /ʔ/ is a glottal stop. It is made when the vocal cords, located in the glottis, are pressed shut so that no air can get through. This sound is heard as the first sound in words beginning with a stressed vowel: *apple, only, each,* etc. It is the first sound we hear in each word in the phrase "oh, oh."

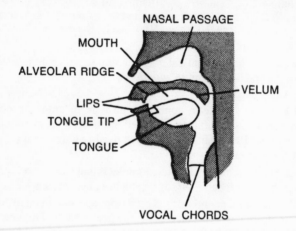

stress   The relative loudness with which speech sounds are uttered. There are four stress phonemes, or relative degrees of loudness: primary ´, secondary ʌ, tertiary ˋ, and weak ˘. Three degrees of stress can occur on one word: *désignàte.* Primary and secondary stress are illustrated in the modifier + noun combinations *hót hòuse, blàck bírd. dàrk roóm.*

string   See TERMINAL STRING.

strong verb   See IRREGULAR VERB.

structural grammar   A system of linguistic description characterized by attention to form and distribution, to the spoken language rather than to writing, to description rather than to prescription. Structural grammar is mainly concerned with phonology (sounds) and morphology (word structure), less with syntax. The study of structural linguistics began in Europe about 1900 with the discovery of the principle of the phoneme and extended to the United States about 1930 with the discovery of the principle of the morpheme. Structural linguistics reached its fullest development in the 1950s with the development of notions of constructions and immediate constituent syntax and with the publication of textbooks for schools and colleges.

REFERENCES: L. Bloomfield, *Language* (New York: Holt, Rinehart and Winston, 1933); W. N. Francis, *The Structure of American English* (New York: Ronald Press, 1958); C. C. Fries, *American English Grammar* (New York: Appleton-Century-Crofts, 1940); _____ , *The Structure of English* (New York: Harcourt, Brace & World, 1952); H. A. Gleason, *Linguistics and English Grammar* (New York: Holt, Rinehart and Winston, 1965); A. A. Hill, *Introduction to Linguistic Structures, From Sound to Sentence in English* (New York: Harcourt, Brace & World, 1958); C. F. Hockett, *A Course in Modern Linguistics* (New York: Macmillan, 1958); Paul Roberts, *Patterns of English* (New York: Harcourt, Brace & World, 1956); E. Sapir, *Language* (New York: Harcourt, Brace & World, 1921; Harvest Book HB7); James Sledd, *A Short Introduction to English Grammar* (Chicago: Scott, Foresman, 1959); N. C. Stageberg, *An Introductory English Grammar* (New York: Holt, Rinehart and Winston, 1965); R. Wells, "Immediate Constituents," *Language,* 23 (1947: 81–117.

structure group word   See FUNCTION WORD.

subject   The subject of a sentence is the noun, pronoun, or nominal structure that usually agrees in number with the verb and, except in inverted sentence order, stands before the verb. The subject is the actor in the active-voice sentence. (See NOMINATIVE CASE.)

subjective complement   A noun or adjective that completes the meaning of a linking verb, and in so doing, modifies, or complements, the subject of that verb: He is *sick.* Bill seems *nice.* Lou became *chairman.*

subjunctive mood   Expressions of wish, doubt, or possibility are said to be in the subjunctive mood.

I wish you *were* here.
If he *were* here, we could leave.
Be it said that he is a good man.

(See MOOD.)

subordinate clause   See DEPENDENT CLAUSE, SUBORDINATION.

subordination   *CG:* The notion that one clause in a sentence has a less important meaning than another clause or clauses in the same sentence. For example, if we want to suggest that the men's beer drinking is less important than their loud singing, we might write a COMPLEX SENTENCE:

The men *who drink beer* sing loudly.
Subord. Clause

The function of subordination is indicated by the word *who.* Three kinds of words indicate subordination in English. Relative pronouns introduce subordinate clauses. *Who* in the sentence above is an example; others are *whose, whom, which, that.* Certain adverbs connect subordinate clauses with main clauses by modifying a word in the main clause. Examples are *when, where, how, whenever, why,* etc.

> The men sing loudly *whenever they drink beer.*
>   Subord. Clause

Subordinating conjunctions also introduce subordinate clauses. These are conjunctions like *since, because, unless, as, for so.*

> *Because the men drink beer,* they sing loudly.
>   Subord. Clause

(See DEPENDENT CLAUSE, COMPLEX SENTENCE.)

REFERENCE: James Sledd, "Coordination Faulty and Subordination Upside Down," *College Composition and Communication* (December, 1956).

subordinator   Subordinators are words like *because, until, if, since, that* whose major function is to subordinate sentences so that they become parts of larger sentences:

> I can't go *because* I don't have any money.
> *Until* you get it you won't come.
> I saw *that* she was ill.

substantive   Nouns, pronouns, and word groups that function as nouns.

suffix   A bound morpheme that attaches to the end of a stem, thus forming a new word or word form. Modern English suffixes are either derivational or inflectional. (See DERIVATIONAL SUFFIX, INFLECTIONAL SUFFIX.)

superfix   A meaningful combination of stresses, the stress pattern on a word or phrase:

> gréenhoùse
> grêen hóuse

superlative degree   The superlative degree of an adjective or adverb is expressed by attaching the suffix *-est* to short words, while long words are preceded by *most: softest, greatest, most agreeable, most comfortable.* Some words, like *happy,* can form the superlative degree either way: *happiest, most happy.* (See COMPARISON, COMPARATIVE DEGREE.)

suppletion   This describes the complete change of stems in a paradigm. *Go* and *be* illustrate suppletion. In the paradigm for *go*

> go goes going went gone

we would expect the past tense form to be *goed.* Instead, the stem /go-/ has been replaced by a different stem /wɛn-/. This change is called suppletion, and *went* is the suppletive form. Looking at the paradigm for *be*

> be am/is/are being was/were been

we note that *am, is, are, was, were* are the suppletive forms. (See PARADIGM.)

suprasegmental phoneme   A term that designates the phenomena of pitch and juncture which are marked above the segments of sound in phonemic transcription. (See INTONATION CONTOUR, PITCH, TERMINAL JUNCTURE.)

surface structure   Surface structure is an abstract string of morphemes which is interpreted into speech or writing. Underlying a surface structure is a deep or conceptual structure that may be the same as or different from the surface structure. The simple, active, declarative surface structure *the + man + see + PAST + Suzie* is related to the identical deep structure through the choice of lexical items and through syntactic rules that rearrange the subject and object Noun Phrases in the surface cluster these morphemes together in groups, constituents, like *the + man* and *see + PAST*. Surface structures that are different from deep structures can be illustrated by (1) *Suzie was seen by the man* and (2) *Shut the door!* The deep structure of (1) is *The man saw Suzie*. These different surface and deep structures are connected by syntactic rules that rearrange the subject and object. Noun Phrases in the surface structure, add a form of the verb *be* and the preposition *by*, and substitute the past participle *seen* for the past tense form *saw*. The deep structure of (2) is *You will shut the door*. The surface structure (2) is connected to the deep structure by syntactic rules that delete *you* and *will*. Surface structures can be interpreted by phonological rules to produce utterances. Or a surface structure can be changed into writing by the application of morphographemic rules. These relationships between surface and deep structure on the one hand and between surface structure and speech and writing can be depicted by this diagram:

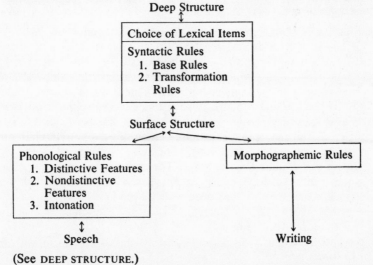

(See DEEP STRUCTURE.)

syllable   A group of phonemes consisting of a vowel alone or a vowel combined with one or more consonants. This group of phonemes is a unit of the word in which it occurs and has its peak of sonority, its carrying power, on the vowel. Here are some English words with their syllabic peaks underlined:

One Syllable:	*me*	/mi̲/
Two Syllables:	*receive*	/rɪsi̲v/
Three Syllables:	*receiving*	/rɪsi̲vɪŋ/
Four Syllables:	*disenchantment*	/dɪsə̲ncæntmə̲nt/
Five Syllables:	*unbelievingly*	/ə̲nbɨli̲vm̲li̲/

(See CLOSED SYLLABLE, OPEN SYLLABLE.)

syllabic consonant   There are four syllabic consonants in English which have sufficient peaks of sonority, carrying power, to occur as syllables by themselves in some pronunciations in which they occur. /m/ is syllabic in the pronunciation of *rob 'em,* in which lips are closed for /b/ and remain closed for /m/: /rabm̩/. /n/ is syllabic in the pronunciation of *glutton,* in which the tongue, in contact with the alveolar ridge for the articulation of /t/, remains there for the articulation of /n/: /glətn̩/. /ŋ/ is syllabic in the pronunciation of *and* in *Jack and Bill,* in which the tongue back, held against the velum for the pronunciation of /k/, remains there as the velum is lowered to produce the syllabic velar nasal phoneme /ŋ/: /jækŋ̩bɪl/. /l/ is syllabic in the pronunciation of *battle,* in which the tongue tip, held against the alveolar ridge for the articulation of /t/, remains there for the pronunciation of /l/: /bætl̩/. (See SYLLABLE.)

synchronic   In linguistics this term denotes the description of a language at a certain limited time in its development, regardless of its past history. (See DIACHRONIC.)

syncopation   This term describes the loss of a sound in a word during the course of its historical development. In Modern English the words *dogs, cats, wishes* are pronounced /dɔgz kæts wɪšɪz/ with three different endings. In the Late Middle English of Chaucer's time they were all pronounced with the same ending: /dɔgəs katəs wɪšəs/. Between Late Middle English and Modern English times the vowel /ə/ syncopated because it occurred in an unstressed syllable, the usual cause of syncopation. The ending *th* for the third-person singular present indicative of verbs, *mākth,* "maketh," *bērth,* "beareth," syncopated during Old English and Middle English times. The verb preterit ending *-ed:* /ɨd/ syncopated after all phonemes except /t/ and /d/ in the fifteenth century. The fact that /ɨd/ was once widely used is indicated by its continued presence in *aged, blessed,* and *learned* when they are used as adjectives: /ejɨd blɛsɪd lərnɨd/.

syntactic construction   A grammatical sequence having only words as its immediate constituents. (See CONSTRUCTION, IMMEDIATE, CONSTITUENT.)

syntax   *CG, Str:* The description of actual written or spoken sentences; a description of the system by which words combine into phrases and clauses and of the ways that these combine into sentences. In structural grammar, phonology is basic, with syntax being the last level of description. *TG:* Syntax is the base of the grammar; it is a part of a theory of grammar. This base consists of three sets of rules: (1) Phrase structure rules, which generate basic sentences rewritten as complex symbols:

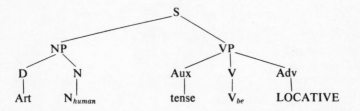

(2) Lexical rules of selection, which substitute words for the complex symbols in the phrase structure string:

Art → the V_{be} → be
N_{human} → man   LOCATIVE → in the house
tense → Present

Lexical rules also assign properties to nouns, pronouns, adjectives, and verbs.

(3) Transformational rules, which add to, rearrange, and subtract from the phrase structure string:

Add:	The old man is in the house.
Rearrange:	Is the old man in the house?
Subtract from:	Yes, the old man is.

(See COMPLEX TRANSFORMATION, SIMPLE TRANSFORMATION, TRANSFORMATION, LEXICAL PROPERTIES.)

REFERENCES: *CG:* M. Bryant, *A Functional English Grammar* (Boston: D. C. Heath, 1950); G. O. Curme, *Syntax* (Boston: D. C. Heath, 1931); R. B. Long, *The Sentence and Its Parts* (Chicago: University of Chicago Press, 1961); *Str:* C. C. Fries, *The Structure of English* (New York: Harcourt, Brace & World, 1952); W. N. Francis, *The Structure of American English* (New York: Ronald Press, 1958); *TG:* See readings under TRANSFORMATIONAL GRAMMAR.

synthetic language   A language in which the relationships among words in a sentence depend mainly upon inflections, the endings on words. Latin, Old English, and modern German are synthetic languages. (See ANALYTIC LANGUAGE, INFLECTIONAL LANGUAGE.)

T

T-unit   A "minimal terminable unit . . . one main clause expanded at any of many different points by structures that are modifiers or complements or substitutes for words in the main clause" (K. W. Hunt, *Grammatical Structures Written at Three Grade Levels* [1965]).

tagmeme   A unit of grammatical arrangement resulting from a slot-class correlation. A *slot* is a grammatical position or function (subject, verbal, object) that is filled by mutually substitutable items, members of a word *class* (nouns and verbs). The utterance *I'd walk* consists of features of the subject-verb slot order, of the classes of words that fill these slots (nouns and verbs), and of phonetic modification—the substitution of *'d* for *would*. Taken alone, none of these three elements has any meaning. But "correlated" they make up a tagmeme whose meaning is that the subject expression "performs" the action of the verb expression.

REFERENCES: W. A. Cook, *Introduction to Tagmemic Analysis* (New York: Holt, Rinehart & Winston, 1969); B. Elson and V. B. Pickett, *Beginning Morphology-Syntax* (Glendale, California: Summer Institute of Linguistics, 1960); R. E. Longacre, "Some Fundamental Insights of Tagmemics," *Language*, 41 (1965) 65–76; Kenneth Pike, *Language in Relation to a Unified Theory of the Structure of Human Behavior* (Glendale, California: Summer Institute of Linguistics, 1954–1960).

tag question   An elliptical inversion of a preceding declarative or imperative sentence which turns the whole sentence into a yes/no question. If the preceding sentence is positive or imperative, the tag question is negative: John has gone, *hasn't he?* Come in, *won't you?* If the preceding declarative sentence is negative, the tag question is positive: John hasn't gone, *has he?* The verb of the tag question is the same as the finite verb of the preceding sentence, if that verb is *be, do,* or a modal auxiliary verb. If a finite verb other than these is used in the preceding sentence, the tag question uses *do:* He likes it, *doesn't he?* He has it, *doesn't he?*

tapped *r*   See FLAPPED *r*.

taxeme   A simple feature of grammatical arrangement; a minimum grammatical feature such as the *order* of words or morphemes (verb follows subject; *-ing* follows *turn*), *selection* (selecting *-ly* to follow *quick* in forming an adverb), *modulation* (strong stress on the first syllable of *quickly;* the rising pitch at the end of "He's walking home?"), or *phonetic modification* ("I would → *I'd*). (See TAGMEME.)

tense   A verb form or combination of verb forms indicating that the time of an action or state of being is past, present, or future. Tense is also an indication of agreement between a finite verb and its subject. This agreement can be in person (*I have; she has*), number (*she has; they have*), or time (*she has; she had*). Traditional grammar describes many phrasal tenses. (See FUTURE TENSE, FUTURE PERFECT TENSE, PAST TENSE, PAST PERFECT TENSE, PRESENT TENSE, PRESENT PERFECT TENSE, PROGRESSIVE TENSE.)

tense vowel   The high vowels /i/ b*ee*t and /u/ p*oo*l are articulated with tense tongue muscles. Lower front and back vowels are lax. (See VOWEL.)

terminal juncture   Junctures are combinations of pitch and pause that signal the connection between parts of a complex utterance or the termination of an utterance. There are three terminal junctures in English. The first one, indicated by ↓, signals the fadeaway of the voice to silence at the end of a statement: *John eats pie* ↓. The second terminal, indicated by ↑, signals the slight rise in pitch at the end of a yes/no question: *Are you here* ↑. The third terminal, indicated by →, is the sustained terminal. It can be most easily recognized as connecting long subjects with their verb: *Most of the people at the game* → *were thrilled by his run* ↓. It also occurs after introductory statements, indicating that the speaker has more to say: *She's a nice girl* → *but. . . .* The predominant characteristic of terminals within utterances is the lengthening of the stressed syllable that precedes them. Contrast the length of time it takes to pronounce *game* in these two sentences:

The game was over ↓
Most of the people at the game → were thrilled by his run

(See INTONATION CONTOUR, SUPRASEGMENTAL.)

terminal string   *TG:* The string of free and bound morphemes produced by application of rewrite rules in the phrase structure grammar. The string is terminal because its symbols cannot be further expanded by any rule in the grammar.

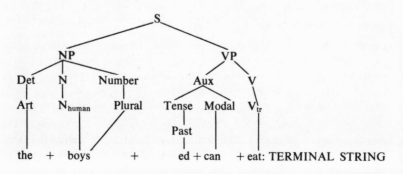

The next step is to apply the obligatory AFFIX TRANSFORMATION:

ed + can ⟹ can + ed ⟹ could

that-clause   In conventional school grammar a *that-clause* is called a noun clause: *I knew that he was sick.* In *TG,* insert sentences are nominalized with *that* for insertion into subject, object, or noun-complement positions in the main sentence.

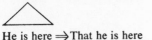

S is strange   I saw S

He is here ⟹ That he is here   He was running ⟹ that he was running

I saw the Car S

He owns the car ⟹ that he owns

(See DEPENDENT CLAUSE, FACTITIVE NOMINAL.)

there transformation   This transformation derives from sentences such as *A man is in the house* a sentence with inverted subject and verb and the expletive word *there* in initial position: *There is a man in the house.* A simplified form of the transformation rule looks like this:

NP + BE + LOCATIVE ADVERB ⟹
There + BE + NP + LOCATIVE ADVERB

This transformation is useful in distinguishing the verb *be* from the linking verbs (*seem, become,* etc.), which cannot be directly followed by a locative adverb, and from other intransitive verbs, which, though they can be followed by a locative adverb (*The man sleeps here*), cannot undergo the there-transformation: **There sleeps a man here.*

thorn   Thorn is the written symbol þ, a rune used in Old English writing. Thorn represented both the voiced and voiceless *th* sound in the initial position, alternating with ð. It disappeared in Late Middle English times, being replaced by *th*. (See ETH, RUNIC WRITING.)

traditional grammar   See SCHOOL GRAMMAR for the usual synonym for this term. There are also the grammars of the scholarly tradition, which reached its peak in Europe in the early years of the twentieth century. The great taxonomic grammars of Otto Jespersen (*A Modern English Grammar,* 7 Vols, 1909–1949), E. Kruisinga (*A Handbook of Present-Day English,* 3 Vols, 1931), H. Poutsma (*A Grammar of Late Modern English,* 5 Vols, 1926–29), and Henry Sweet (*A New English Grammar,* 1891–98) exemplify this tradition. The work of George Curme (*Parts of Speech and Accidence,* 1935; *Syntax,* 1931) reflects this tradition in America. R. W. Zandvoort, *A Handbook of English Grammar* (3rd ed., 1966), and G. Scheurweghs, *Present-Day*

English Syntax: A Survey of Sentence Patterns (1959), are the most recent works in this illustrious genre of grammars.

transcription   The conversion of the sounds of speech into writing, into a written form in which each letter stands for only one sound. There are two types of transcription, phonetic and phonemic. Phonetic transcription notes all the allophones, variants, of a given phoneme. In phonetic transcription, phones are written within brackets [   ]. For example, the allophones of the phoneme /r/ are written

trilled:	[ř]	Scottish *red*
voiced fricative:	[ɹ]	U.S. *dream*
voiceless fricative:	[ɹ̥]	*tree*
devoiced:	[ɾ̥]	*pray*
flapped:	[ɾ]	British *hurry*

In phonemic transcription, the kind used in this glossary, we use the same character for all the allophones of a given phoneme, and the phonemes are written within slant lines; *r* and all its allophones are written /r/. There are four major systems of phonemic transcription: the system used in *Webster's Third International Dictionary* (1961); the system developed by K. L. Pike and C. C. Fries of the University of Michigan (about 1947); the system used by Trager and Smith in *An Outline of English Structure* (1951); and the International Phonetic Alphabet. These systems are compared below. The IPA Alphabet given here is that found in Kenyon and Knott, *A Pronouncing Dictionary of American English* (10th edition). This version is the widest dissemination of the IPA in a form adapted to the sounds of American English.

Webster 3	Pike-Fries	Trager-Smith	IPA	
ē	i	i	i	
i	ɪ	ɪ	ɪ	
ā	e	e	e	
e	ɛ	ɛ	ɛ	
a	æ	æ	æ	
ə	ə	ə	ə	VOWELS
ər	ər	ɚ	ɚ	AND
ä	a	a	a	DIPHTHONGS
ü	u	u	u	
u̇	ʊ	ʊ	ʊ	
ō	o	o	o	
ȯ	ɔ	ɔ	ɔ	
ī	aɪ	ay	aɪ	
au̇	aʊ	aw	aʊ	
ȯi	ɔɪ	oy	ɔɪ	

Webster 3	Pike-Fries	Trager-Smith	IPA	
p	p	p	p	
b	b	b	b	
t	t	t	t	
d	d	d	d	
k	k	k	k	
g	g	g	g	
ch	č	č	tʃ	
j	ǰ	ǰ	dʒ	
f	f	f	f	
v	v	v	v	CONSONANTS
th	θ	θ	θ	
<u>th</u>	ð	ð	ð	
s	s	s	s	
z	z	z	z	
sh	š	š	ʃ	
zh	ž	ž	ʒ	
h	h	h	h	
m	m	m	m	
n	n	n	n	
ŋ	ŋ	ŋ	ŋ	
l	l	l	l	
r	r	r	r	
y	y	y	j	GLIDES
w	w	w	w	

transform *TG:* A transform is a structure that is the result of the process of transformation and is, thus, related to the sentence from which it is derived. Sometimes a transform is another sentence. For example, the passive sentence

The dog was patted by the man.

is a transform derived from the active voice sentence

The man patted the dog.

Sometimes a transform is only part of a sentence. *The man's patting the dog* is a gerund transform derived from *The man patted the dog*. When a transform is part of a sentence it can be embedded in a main-clause sentence:

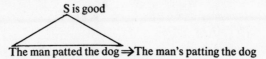

Readout: The man's patting the dog is good.

(See COMPLEX TRANSFORMATION, MULTIPLE-COMPLEX TRANSFORMATION.)

transformation *TG:* The process that derives from one syntactic structure a different yet related one. Transformations are of two kinds, simple and complex. (For examples of simple transformations see AFFIX TRANSFORMATION, DO-TRANSFORMATION, IMPERATIVE MOOD, NEGATIVE TRANSFORMATION, PASSIVE TRANSFORMATION, SIMPLE TRANSFORMATION, THERE-TRANSFORMATION. For examples of complex transformations see COMPLEX TRANSFORMATION, CONSTITUENT SENTENCE, DEPENDENT CLAUSE, DOUBLE-BASE TRANSFORMATION, MULTIPLE-COMPLEX TRANSFORMATION, NOUN-COMPLEMENT POSITION, PRO-FORM, RECURSIVE-COMPLEX TRANSFORMATION.) Transformations are one of the three parts of the syntactic component of a transformational grammar. The other two parts are the set of basic sentences and the lexicon. (See DICTIONARY, LEXICON, SENTENCE PATTERN, SYNTAX, TRANSFORMATIONAL GRAMMAR.)

transformational grammar In one sense, this is a theory of grammar that suggests the abstract ability of a native speaker to produce an infinite number of sentences. This grammar predicts all of the grammatical sentences available to the native speaker. Transformational grammar differs from conventional classroom grammar and structural grammar in that it neither analyzes particular sentences nor describes speech production. The complete theory of transformational grammar consists of a syntactic component (phrase-structure, lexicon, transformations), a semantic component (a dictionary and rules that show the relationships among dictionary meanings), and a phonological component, which consists of pronunciation and spelling rules. This model of the grammar dates from the publication of Noam Chomsky's *Syntactic Structures* (1957) and has more recently been modified by Chomsky (*Aspects of the Theory of Syntax,* 1965) and others. (See DICTIONARY and the references under GENERATIVE GRAMMAR and TRANSFORMATION.)

REFERENCES: E. Bach and R. T. Harms (eds.), *Universals in Linguistic Theory* (New York: Holt, Rinehart and Winston, 1968); N. R. Cattell, *The New English Grammar* (Cambridge, Mass.: MIT Press, 1969); J. A. Fodor and J. J. Katz (eds.), *The Structure of Language: Readings in the Philosophy of Language* (Englewood Cliffs: Prentice-Hall, 1964), pp. 50–118, 119–136, 211–245, 384–389, 547–578; R. A. Jacobs and P. S. Rosenbaum, *English Transformational Grammar* (Waltham, Mass.: Blaisdell, 1968); J. J. Katz, *The Philosophy of Language* (New York: Harper & Row, 1966); _____ and P. M. Postal, *An Integrated Theory of Linguistic Descriptions* (Cambridge, Mass.: MIT Press, 1964); A. Koutsoudas, *Writing Transformational Grammars* (New York: McGraw-Hill, 1966); G. Lakoff, *Irregularity in Syntax* (New York: Holt, Rinehart and Winston, 1970); R. W. Langacker, *Language and Its Structure* (New York: Harcourt, Brace and World, 1968); D. T. Langendoen, *Essentials of English Grammar* (New York: Holt, Rinehart and Winston, 1969); R. B. Lees, *The Grammar of English Nominalizations* (Bloomington, Ind.: Indiana University, 1963); P. M. Postal, *Constituent Structure: A Study of Contemporary Models of Syntactic Description* (The Hague: Mouton, 1964); _____, "Underlying and Superficial Linguistic Structure," *Harvard Educational Review,* 34 (Spring, 1964): 246–66; J. Emig, J. Fleming, and H. Popp (eds.), *Language and Learning* (New York: Harcourt, Brace and World, 1966), pp. 153–175; R. Stockwell, B. Partee, *et al., Integration of Transformational Theories on English Syntax.* 2 vols. (Los Angeles: UCLA Bookstore, 1969); J. M. Williams, *The New English* (New York: The Free Press, 1970).

transformational rule   See RULE OF GRAMMAR, REWRITE RULE.

transitive verb   A verb that takes a direct object (Jim drinks *milk*), an indirect object (John gave *Bill* the key), and object complements (They elected Andy *president*). (See FACTITIVE VERB, OBJECT COMPLEMENT.)

transposition   This describes a kind of word order pattern, found mainly in the poetry and prose of earlier historical stages of English, in which objects are transposed before verbs (*A sorry song we might all sing*) or verbs are transposed before auxiliary verbs (*The people assembled were*). (See INVERSION.)

tree diagram.   *TG:* This represents the syntactic structure of a sentence. It shows the word order of the sentence, indicates the relationship among the constituents of the sentence, and explicitly labels these constituents.

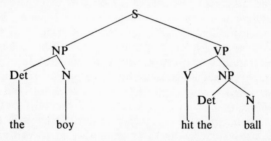

(See DIAGRAM, INTERMEDIATE STRUCTURE, PHRASE MARKER.)

trilled *r*   The trilled *r* is made by several taps of the tongue tip against the alveolar ridge, as in Scottish, Welsh, Spanish, and the Slavic languages, or by the back of the tongue against the uvula, as in German. (See TRANSCRIPTION.)

U

ultimate constituent   *Str:* In morphology the ultimate constituents are the morphemes of which a word is composed:

$$\underline{\text{life} \mid \text{less} \mid \text{ness}}$$

In syntax the ultimate constituents are usually the individual words of the utterance. (See IMMEDIATE CONSTITUENT.)

umlaut   The change in an accented low or back vowel (*a, o, u*) brought about by anticipation of a high front vowel such as /i: ɪ y/ in the following syllable. Evidences in Modern English of this "i-umlaut" can be seen in the pairs *goose : geese, man : men.* The presence of *i* in the second syllable of the Primitive Germanic **gosiz* brought about the fronting of /o:/ eventually to /i:/. The presence of *i* in the second syllable of Primitive German **manni* eventually brought about the fronting of /a/ to /ɛ/. The pair *louse : lice,* from Old English *lūs : lȳs,* illustrates the fronting of /u:/ to /y:/. Umlaut should not be confused with ABLAUT (See FRONTING.)

usage   The customary manners of speaking or writing a language; the lexical, grammatical, and phonological choices we make. The term also denotes a particular example of a customary manner of speaking or writing, such as the use of the double negative. While a description of levels and varieties of usage is very complex (See John S. Kenyon, "Cultural Levels and Functional Varieties of English," in Harold B. Allen [ed.], *Readings in Applied English Linguistics* [2nd ed., 1964], pp. 294-301), we can say that there are two general varieties of English usage, Standard and Nonstandard. Standard English is that used by educated, cultivated people to communicate in speech and writing. Because it is the language of influential people, its use is socially advantageous. There are three general varieties of Standard English: *formal* (used in serious writing and in formal speeches), *informal* (used in books and magazines intended for the general reader), and *colloquial* (conversation and in writing where the conversational idiom is desired). The dividing line between Standard and Nonstandard English is not clear, since usage is frequently shared between the two. Nonstandard English is infrequently used by Standard English speakers, since some of its expressions, such as the double negative, put the speaker at a social and economic disadvantage. But the fact that the dividing line between Standard and Nonstandard English is not always clear should caution us to regard Nonstandard usage as different from, and not necessarily inferior to, Standard usage. (See CULTURAL LEVEL OF USAGE, FUNCTIONAL VARIETY OF USAGE.)

REFERENCES: M. Bryant, *Current American Usage* (New York: Funk & Wagnalls, 1962); M. Joos, *The Five Clocks* (Bloomington, Indiana: *International Journal of American Linguistics* 28(1962), No. 2; New York: Harcourt, Brace & World, 1968); Bergen and Cornelia Evans, *A Dictionary of Contemporary American Usage* (New York: Random House, 1957).

usage label   The purpose of usage labels, which sometimes appear with definitions in dictionaries, is to identify the general nature of the context in which the word is ordinarily used. Usage labels are usually of three kinds: stylistic (*slang, nonstand.*), temporal (*archaic, obs.*), and regional (*dial., dial. Brit., New. Eng., Midland*). (See DICTIONARY.)

V

velar stop   /k/ and /g/ are velar stops. (See STOP.)

verb   *CG:* A verb names an action or state of being. Verbs are of two kinds: auxiliary (helping) and full (main). *Str., TG:* The verb is a part of speech class whose members exhibit certain formal, distributional, and semantic characteristics.

(1) *Formal* (*a*) Inflection: the verb is capable of inflection for the present tense third person singular {-s} *learns;* past tense {-d} *learned;* past participle {-d} *learned* or *-en chosen;* and the present participle {-ing} *learning.* (*b*) Derivation: verbs may be derived from bound stems, nouns, and adjectives by the addition of derivational suffixes such as *-ate* (orchestrate), *ize* (idolize), *-fy* (beautify), *-ish* (furnish), *-en* (blacken). (*c*) Agreement: the finite verb exhibits the tense and person or number concord with its subject in the present or past tense. The present and past participles do not show concord with a subject because the tense marker attaches to the first verb in the verb phrase, whether the phrase contains only a main verb (*He runs*) or one or more auxiliaries: *He will run, He has run, He is running,* etc.

(2) *Distributional:* the verb patterns after the noun phrase subject. (See the transformational grammar description of SENTENCE PATTERN.) On the basis of the kind of complement a verb requires, the kinds of transformations a sentence can undergo, and the freedom with which a sentence can accept verbs, there are at least five kinds of verbs: transitive, intransitive, mid, linking, and *be.*

(3) *Semantic:* The semantic characteristics of the verb tell what the subject does, is, or has. The semantic characteristic describes an action or state of being. But it is frequently difficult to define verbs by their semantic characteristics alone. (See INTRANSITIVE VERB, LEXICAL PROPERTIES, TENSE, TRANSITIVE VERB.)

REFERENCES: M. Joos, *The English Verb: Form and Meanings* (Madison: University of Wisconsin Press, 1964); A. G. Juilland and J. Macris, *The English Verb System* ('s-Gravenhage: Mouton, 1962); J. Svartik, *On Voice in the English Verb* ('s-Gravenhage: Mouton, 1966); W. F. Twaddell, *The English Verb Auxiliaries* (Providence: Brown University Press, 1960).

verb-headed construction   *Str:* This term denotes a construction in which a verb is the headword: quickly *ran* : quickly *ran* home yesterday; has quickly *run* the race. (See HEADWORD.)

verb phrase   *CG:* This consists of the main verb and its auxiliary verb(s). *TG:* This is composed of auxiliary material and the main verb: VP → Aux + MV. The auxiliary consists of present or past tense and, optionally, a modal verb and/or *have* and/or *be:* Aux → Tense (modal) (have + en) (be + ing). The main verb can be variously subclassified. (See MID-VERB, VERB.)

verbal   *CG:* This term denotes the infinitives of verbs and the verb + *ing* and the verb + *ed* when they function as nouns and adjectives. The *gerund* is the verb + *ing* in its noun function: *Skiing* is fun. He likes *swimming*. The participle is the verb + *ing* and verb + *ed* in its adjective function: We heard *running* water. *Used* in several ways, the verb is an *interesting* word. The base form of the verb preceded by *to* is called the *infinitive*. Infinitives are also verbals and function as nouns (*To learn* is good), adjectives (John had a wish *to travel*), and adverbs (He waited *to see* Sue). *TG:* It is apparent that verbs and adjectives have some properties in common in the deep structure of sentences. They are both considered as verbals, marked ⟨+VB⟩, and their differences are marked by the features ⟨+V⟩ for verbs and ⟨−V⟩ for adjectives. (See LEXICAL PROPERTIES.)

Verner's Law   Like Grimm's Law, Verner's Law is a simple statement describing systematic changes in pronunciation. In 1875 Karl Verner, a Danish scholar, explained the presence of the voiced fricative sounds *b, d, g* in Germanic languages in which, according to Grimm's Law, we should expect to find voiceless sounds, *p, t, k*. Verner also explained the principle of *rhotacism* (r-ing) in which the Indo-European *s* develops in Germanic to *z* and *r*. The following diagram will show Verner's modification of one stage of Grimm's Law:

GRIMM			*VERNER*	*EXAMPLE*
I-E	*Gmc*		*Gmc*	
p	→ f	→	b = OE /v/	a li*fe*/ to li*v*e
				a grie*f*/ to grie*v*e
t	→ þ (th) →		d	dea*th*... dea*d*
k	→ x (h) →		g	Example may be found in the two pronunciations of the Modern English *exit*: /ɛksɪt/; /ɛgzɪt/

Rhotacism can be stated as follows:

I-E	*Gmc*		
s	⟶ s → z → r		OE wæ*s*, wæron → MnE wa*s*, we*r*e

Verner concluded that these voiced sounds occurred because stress was not on the first syllable, that this voicing occurred before the Germanic stress shift to the first syllable. (See FIRST CONSONANT SHIFT, GRIMM'S LAW.)

vocative case   *CG:* In fully inflected languages the case that marks the person being addressed. In the Latin *miserere, Domine* ("have mercy, O Lord") *Domine* is marked for the vocative case. Even in relatively uninflected languages like English, school grammar books sometimes consider *Joe* in *Joe, come here* as being in the vocative case.

voice of verbs   See ACTIVE VOICE, PASSIVE VOICE.

voiced voiceless   A voiced sound is one made when breath forced from the lungs vibrates the vocal cords. All vowels are voiced sounds, as are some consonants (m, n, b, d, g, z, etc.). Voiceless sounds are those made without vibration of the vocal cords. Some consonants are voiceless (s, t, k, p, etc.). (See STOP, VOWEL.)

vowel   Voiced sounds produced by the breath passing through the opened mouth with relatively little obstruction by the speech organs. The term also names the written letters *a, e, i, o, u*. Generally speaking, vowels are characterized according to the height of the tongue in the mouth and according to its front-back position in the mouth. Thus, high vowels are produced with the tongue relatively high in the mouth; low vowels have the tongue relatively low, and mid vowels have the tongue between high and low position. Front, central, and back vowels are produced with the tongue in these positions from the front to the back of the mouth. All of this can be represented on what is called a vowel quadrangle. This is a representation of the tongue positions in the mouth:

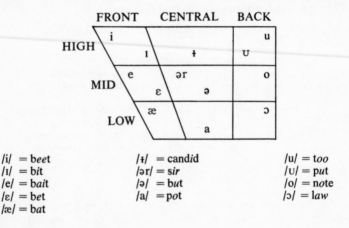

/i/ = b*ee*t	/ɨ/ = cand*i*d	/u/ = t*oo*
/ɪ/ = b*i*t	/ər/ = s*ir*	/ʊ/ = p*u*t
/e/ = b*ai*t	/ə/ = b*u*t	/o/ = n*o*te
/ɛ/ = b*e*t	/a/ = p*o*t	/ɔ/ = l*a*w
/æ/ = b*a*t		

(See DISTINCTIVE FEATURES.)

W

wave theory   In 1872 Johannes Schmidt postulated the *wave hypothesis*. Schmidt demonstrated that similarities can be found between any two branches of Indo-European, and these similarities are most frequent in the case of branches that lie geographically nearest to each other. Thus, languages that originate from a parent language spread from this parent in all directions, and changes in languages spread in the same way—like waves moving out from the point at which a stone lands in a pool. In accounting for linguistic differentiations, the wave theory stands in contrast to the splitting process implied by the FAMILY TREE THEORY. (See FAMILY TREE THEORY, GLOTTOCHRONOLOGY.)

wh-clause   *TG:* A Wh-clause is a sentence which has been transformed to contain a wh-word so that this sentence can be inserted into a nominal, noun-complement, or adverbial position in a main-clause sentence.

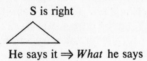

S is right

He says it ⇒ *What* he says

Readout: What he says is right.

The boy S is asleep.

You know the boy ⇒ *who* you know

Readout: The boy who you know is asleep.

He stays S

He lives there ⇒ *where* he lives

Readout: He stays where he lives.

Any structure in an insert sentence can be changed to a wh-word and moved to the front of the sentence to produce a wh-clause. But notice that the use of wh-words to make nominal, noun-complement, or adverbial clauses does not cause inversion of the subject and finite verb since these clauses do not produce questions. (See WH-QUESTION, WH-WORD.)

wh-question   *Str., TG:* So-called because it begins with a word containing the letters *w* and *h: who, whom, whose, what, which, why, where, when, how,* and sometimes their compounds ending in *-ever.* The *wh*-question is an information question, that is, it requires information rather than *yes* or *no* for an answer. Any element, any structure, in a yes/no question can be changed to a *wh*-word and moved to the front of the sentence to produce an information question:

Yes/No Question: Will John give his paper in the seminar tomorrow?
Question the Subject: Who will give his paper in the seminar tomorrow?
Question the Object: What will John give in the seminar tomorrow?
Question the Determiner of the Object: Whose paper will John give. . . ?
Question the Locative Adverb: Where will John give his paper tomorrow?
Question the Time Adverb: When will John give his paper in the seminar?

(See QUESTION.)

wh-word   See WH-QUESTION.

word   In writing, a word is understood to be a sequence of letters with or without a hyphen, sometimes with space within it (as in *snow tires*), always with space before it and after it. From the point of view of morphemics, a word is said to be a free form (it can be used alone, uncombined with any other forms) having only one base, either free (*annoy*-ance) or bound (*dissent*). Compound words consist of two or more bases (*baseball, brother-in-law, bluebird*). (See BASE, BOUND MORPHEME, FREE MORPHEME.)

word order   This term describes the order in which words may occur in a phrase (*gave him the car*) or in a sentence (*The dog barked ferociously*). (See INVERSION, TRANSPOSITION.)

wynn   The runic character Þ used in Old English writing. It represented /w/. (See RUNIC WRITING.)

Y

yes/no question   Yes/no questions are so-called because they elicit an answer *yes* or *no*. They are of two kinds. The yes/no question in statement form asks the question by means of the intonation contour 233↑: ²You're³ here³↑. The yes/no question in question form has the same intonation contour but the question is signaled by grammar—the inversion of subject and verb: ²Are you³here³↑. (See INTONATION CONTOUR, TERMINAL JUNCTURE, QUESTION, WH-QUESTION.)

yogh   A written symbol. In Old English times its shape was ȝ and it stood for the voiced velar stop /g/ before consonants (*glæd*), initially before back vowels (*gōs*), and initially before mutated front vowels (*gēs*). In the combination *ng* (*bringan*) it represented the sound in Modern English *linger:* /ŋg/. Initially before *e, i,* and *y,* yogh represented /y/ (*gecoren, giftian, gydd*). In other positions in Old English yogh represented the voiced velar fricative /ɣ/: /draȝan/. In Early Middle English its shape was ȝ and it was used for the sound of *y* (ȝelde(n)) and for the voiceless velar fricative /x/; *cniȝt,* spelled *gh* in the Late Middle English of Chaucer's time and in Modern English.

Z

zero allomorph   A variant of a morpheme. If no actual sound change is evident, if there is zero variation in sound, the zero allomorph has been added. For example, the plural of *bear* and *deer* is identical with the singular. When these words are used as plurals, it is said that the plural is formed by the addition of a zero allomorph of the plural morpheme {-s}. (See ALLOMORPH, MORPHOLOGICAL CONDITIONING.)